T0115110

Feng Shui Beyond Boundaries

Feng Shui Beyond Boundaries

Your Happy Days Begin Here and Now

Vee Huynh

iUniverse, Inc.
Bloomington

Feng Shui Beyond Boundaries
Your Happy Days Begin Here and Now

Copyright © 2012 by Vee Huynh

All rights reserved. No part of this book may be used or reproduced by any means, graphic, electronic, or mechanical, including photocopying, recording, taping or by any information storage retrieval system without the written permission of the publisher except in the case of brief quotations embodied in critical articles and reviews.

iUniverse books may be ordered through booksellers or by contacting:

iUniverse
1663 Liberty Drive
Bloomington, IN 47403
www.iuniverse.com
1-800-Authors (1-800-288-4677)

Because of the dynamic nature of the Internet, any web addresses or links contained in this book may have changed since publication and may no longer be valid. The views expressed in this work are solely those of the author and do not necessarily reflect the views of the publisher, and the publisher hereby disclaims any responsibility for them.

Any people depicted in stock imagery provided by Thinkstock are models, and such images are being used for illustrative purposes only.

Certain stock imagery © Thinkstock.

ISBN: 978-1-4759-6215-4 (sc)
ISBN: 978-1-4759-6216-1 (hc)
ISBN: 978-1-4759-6217-8 (e)

Library of Congress Control Number: 2012921693

Printed in the United States of America

iUniverse rev. date: 12/11/2012

Dedication

For Phuong, Hannah, and Karen—
and anyone who's ready to make a change in destiny.

Contents

How You Will Benefit from This Book

A journey of a thousand miles must begin with a single step.
—**Lao Tzu**

Congratulations! You have made one of the greatest decisions of your life, and perhaps the most significant investment you'll ever make for yourself and your loved ones. What you have in your hands holds the magic to your happiness; it's a new start that promises joy and sweet dreams.

You are about to embark on a leap of faith, undertaking a new venture with a clear vision to begin a new life. In other words, you are about to redefine your future.

The purpose of this book is both to provide you with feng shui's potent secret formulas and to offer suggestions for using them to create your new destiny. The book is packed with ancient theories backed by modern science about the power of mind energy. This vital information will help you escape from any of your current undesirable situations and enter that pivotal moment when you change your life. You'll get the real wisdom you need to resolve conflicts in every area of your life, including your health, your relationships, your career and education, your wealth and power, and even your reputation.

This book is filled with spiritual wisdom to awaken the buddha-nature that is seated deep within each of us. It will help broaden the windows from which you view the world so you see life from a different perspective, looking within to find solutions to your problems rather than focusing on the problems themselves.

Life can be as difficult as swimming in treacherous ocean waters, but you can stroke your way back to land with ease when you understand how to identify the three main causes of your struggles.

Your thoughts comprise your mind energy, which is the most powerful force in the universe. It is also essential to successful feng shui practices—a fact that most people ignore or simply do not know. The quality of your thoughts affects the results of feng shui as well as how quickly you achieve those results. With this book, you will gain deeper insight into this remarkable and wondrous power. What you'll discover will help you cut through waves of useless emotions; overcome endless walls of worries and obstacles; and eradicate conflicting internal energies that can stop you from moving forward, dampening your spirits and diminishing your dreams.

You'll gain invaluable techniques that will help you finally put an end to unhealthy habits that have been ruling your life for years. Whether you're trying to quit smoking, drinking, overeating, or gambling, this book will give you insight into the hidden reasons behind your unhealthy behavior. The best part of this type of healing is that it's as natural as it can be—and I promise you that there will be no struggle or withdrawal in the process either. At the same time, you'll be able to effectively identify potential bad habits and prevent them from developing.

Learn to ask and trust the mighty power of your intuition for answers and guidance. Find out how to face your fears with conviction and overcome them in difficult situations. With this book you will learn how to gather information and build your own map of energy flow, or *chi*, in your home, business, or office. That information will help you pinpoint where good and bad energies are located so you can take the necessary steps to strengthen or correct them.

Everyone can benefit from the information in this book—information you don't get from formal education. It's highly beneficial for young readers who are just beginning life's long journey, with so much to be discovered and learned. It will prepare them emotionally when they're facing a crisis or experiencing one of life's darker moments. Adult readers will find this book fascinating as they read about circumstances that mirror their own daily lives—and as they consider for the first time what might have been the effect on their lives if they had made some choices differently. Those people whose lives have been disrupted by the economy will find hope for breaking out of this dreadful moment. Older folks still seeking inner peace and tranquility in their lives will discover the joy that comes from balanced living. Life is filled with magic and miracles, but your mind must be ready to see them.

We are all pursuing happiness, but some of us get lost in the hunt when we chase one of the world's many temptations. When our ego takes control, we've lost our understanding of our true nature; we become disconnected from our inner world. This feng shui book is intended to stimulate your true self, enlighten your spirit, and heighten your senses, taking you to a deeper and higher level of thinking so you can discover your true, natural state of happiness. Its purpose is to accompany you on your lifelong, adventure into the unknown. Not only will it help you understand the true art of living, but it will also help you gain clarity to discern your ideal path to living purposefully and meaningfully, filling in what is missing and lessening what is already full.

Introduction

The world isn't coming to an end, but nowadays it seems like it is—there's just something in the air. Differences among nations are threatening peace around the world, and the financial meltdown in 2008 certainly did enormous damage to many families and individuals. Some unfortunate souls have found that their lives have forever changed. Perhaps you're one of them: you may have lost your home, your business, or your life savings. Your family may be one of the many facing foreclosure. Maybe you're unemployed—or you have a job, but you don't know if you'll have one tomorrow. And just when you think things can't get any worse, they do. Why? Because the negative energy inside you has grown stronger than ever, and the problems won't end until you make a change within.

Some people escaped the financial crisis only to find themselves immersed in some other difficulty. Their lives may have been affected by the recent onslaught of natural disasters: earthquakes, storms, floods, mudslides, and fires. And then there are individuals and couples, young and old, who may be financially secure but who have problems in their relationships, either at work or within their family circle. Members of the younger generation, especially, may find it hard to deal with everyday life in this fast-moving society where everything is expected to happen instantly: instant gratification of needs, instant results, instant wealth, etc. Without patience and proper guidance, they will find that their lives are as difficult as swimming in a rough ocean.

Our world is impermanent, and so are we. Everything in the universe is constantly changing from one state to another. Change is both immediate and imminent, and everyone experiences it differently. Some people are living in joy, while others are living in hellish agony.

What if I told you there's way out for those of you who are going through a crisis at the moment—would you give it a try? If you could learn the key to living a happy life even in turbulent conditions, would you care to find out what it is? What if I said your fate is about to change for the better—would you be interested? You see, to change your luck, first you must change your mind-set, your attitudes, and your views. Once you have decided to do so and make those changes within, that negative energy takes on another form and emerges as positive energy. Positive and negative energies cannot expand within you simultaneously: according to the natural law of the universe, only one can take precedence at any given moment. The effect on your life will be phenomenal.

Did you know that if you live life according to Tao—known as "the Way" or "the Middle Way" in Buddhism—you can dramatically change your fate in life? Your present actions and accumulated good or bad deeds—your merits or demerits—can change your destiny.

True, certain elements of your fate are set the moment you are born, predetermining your life's course. For example, fate determines when your life will begin and end, and whether you will be born a genius or physically impaired (or maybe both). What kind of family you'll have, how rich or poor you'll be—all these things are predetermined based on your karma, your deeds, and your actions from your past two lifetimes. In Buddhism it's called the law of cause and effect; in the West it's called the golden rule. But once you understand the reasons for your creation and abide by universal rules, fate will gradually lessen its powers over you, and you will then be in control of your own destiny.

The truth is, you have the ability to make your choices, as emphasized in Zen or dharma, a Buddhist teaching. You can decide on the course of your life right now by altering your thoughts, your actions, and your attitude toward life.

There are many individuals who have refused to let their physical condition control their lives or constrain their ability to perform tasks. Instead, they took control of their own destiny and altered their fate.

Here's an excellent example we all can look to for inspiration:

This person has suffered from neuromuscular dystrophy since young adulthood; the disease has left him paralyzed and incapable of speech. He can communicate only through a voice synthesizer hooked up to a computer. Yet his writing—particularly his book *A Brief History of Time*—has earned him worldwide recognition. He is renowned physicist Stephen Hawking.

In the first part of this book, I will elaborate in detail on various perspectives on feng shui from ancient Chinese wisdom as well as modern metaphysics. I think both help us understand this complex topic, much of which is still a mystery, and they can help us learn to see the physical world not only with our senses but with our intuition. At the basic level, this wisdom serves as inspiration for self-examination; through heightened self-awareness and continuous improvement, we can come to find true meaning in daily living. Young readers will find that the insights in this book are like messages from their personal guiding angel, assisting them along the way to a happy lifelong journey. And undoubtedly, the real wisdom they will gain will help them overcome any rough spots in their life.

Feng shui functions at two energetic levels—mental and physical. At the mental level, we must prepare our frame of mind so it presents the optimum conditions for good results. We should (1) look within to release blockages; (2) sharpen our visions and goals to ensure clarity; and (3) take necessary action.

At the physical level, our body responds to and mingles with the surrounding environment, which was created by our mind in the first place. The mind and body are interdependent, as signified by the Tao's yin-yang symbol: one defines the other, and neither can exist without the other.

Once you have worked to change from the inside out, feng shui can enhance your power of intention by strengthening it and shifting it from negative to positive—allowing events, situations, people, and resources to appear in your life and propel you toward your goals and dreams.

Everything we consider here can be used as a catalyst—a trigger, if you will—to gather your inner energy and strength so that you can break out of your old patterns and let new ones emerge. It's a way of thinning out older layers of suppressed negative energies (emotions). Your new attitude, coupled with the implementation of feng shui, can help you reconnect with your true nature (your buddha-nature). At the most fundamental level, changing your fate is all about your ideas toward life; your outer world is only a physical manifestation of your innermost thoughts. It all begins with your mind energy.

The method I prescribe here is the same method I used to transform my vision into this book. The energy is the same type that was operating in your subconscious to attract your attention to this book—only now you will have a clearer understanding of its powers and its principles, so that you, too, can put them to work for you. I learned about this fascinating notion in Joe Vitale's book *Life's Missing Instruction Manual*.

Part I

Chapter 1

The Intangible Powers of Feng Shui

Your sacred space is where you find yourself again and again.
—Joseph Campbell

We're constantly affected by the many life-force energies we encounter every day—including our own chi that comes in contact with the surrounding environment, thus affecting our mood, behavior, and luck. The human body naturally functions like a receiver, picking up all energies that cross its path. The weather, other people, news, events, food and beverages—all these things can have an immediate effect on our mental state. Other energies such as lighting, colors, textures, sounds, and smells, can be subtler, affecting us gradually.

Failure to understand these truths that underpin the "magical" world of feng shui is the reason why some people haven't experienced its full powers. The results of feng shui vary from one person to another; some people don't experience any results at all. Why? Because they mistakenly believe that they can solve their problems by simply placing certain objects here and there. But without a proper understanding of feng shui, without putting thoughts and feelings into the process, by not interacting with the power, it becomes weak and ineffective, just as your home may not feel like "home" if your chi-energy is missing from it. You and your belongings define the character of your home. Think about it: you can sense the difference in energy between a relative's house and a friend's. Even within the same house, the energy changes from your parents' room to your sibling's room to your own.

Feng shui isn't just about the placement or rearrangement of things in our immediate environment to get rid of bad luck or to attract what we want. It's a lot more than that—its principles extend far beyond walls and other physical barriers. In fact, if you were to learn just the physical placement aspects of feng shui, you'd have learned a partial truth. The proper practice of feng shui has as much to do with our inner selves as with our outer environment, if not more: our reality has turned ugly because of impure thoughts on the inside. We must stop the cluttered energy flows from both worlds—internal and external—since they are tied closely together, as represented by the Tao's yin-yang symbol of balance.

All our wants and desires must originate in our hearts and minds. Because our mind is the birthplace of all our physical conditions and realities, the place where all our creations begin, it must be tended and trained with proper thinking. Our ideas and dreams are being formed at this level, so it's imperative that our state of mind represents a healthy environment in which the creative process can begin to take shape. Unfortunately, the mind is also the birthplace of all human conflict, including self-destruction. It's important, therefore, that we recognize how our mental patterns cause us to behave as we do. That's why I've dedicated the first part of this book to discussing these issues. I'll explain how to take control of your emotions as you go through daily life, and I'll provide insight into the power of the human mind. The more we know about our mind, the more effectively we can use it to our benefit. I will also introduce you to ancient wisdom that can help you achieve the changes you want in your life.

The human body is a sacred space for the soul, a temporary shelter for the spirit. It's also a mechanism for the spirit to make contact with beings in other realms. You see, without our bodies, individual humans wouldn't exist, and without our spirits, we would have no need for a body. Don't you think your spiritual house, your human body, is just as critical as your physical house? This is why we must achieve good feng shui at both levels, internal and external, in order to experience its true power.

In every game, mental strength is as crucial to winning as physical strength. When we have a better understanding of our mental strengths, weaknesses, and patterns, we can resolve any problems in our game much more effectively and quickly. Likewise, we can succeed in life far more than we'd ever hoped when we use feng shui as a tool for reinforcing our intentions, sharpening our focus, and coordinating our efforts so that we can achieve our goals with confidence.

You can prepare yourself for a change of luck by learning how to identify and fine-tune your mind-set. When you read this book you'll gain insight into the wisdoms of Buddhism, which will prepare you mentally, while the secret feng shui techniques used by ancient masters in the art of harmonious living will help you deepen your intention at the physical level. You will become more aware and appreciative of nature's subtle energies, which are all around us. You will also learn the critical feng shui evaluation process and even create your own feng shui magic.

The second part this book will help you practice feng shui to maximize its true potential. I'll discuss how to assess your surrounding energies methodically, using an authentic Flying Stars feng shui system derived from the classic I Ching, "the Book of Changes." I'll reveal the Eight Characters (Bazhi) method, a traditional feng shui system of astrology that helps you refine your analysis for how to maximize the energies in your personal space.

The Birthplace of Your Creation

The mind is everything. What you think you become ... Everything is based on mind, is led by mind, is fashioned by mind. If you speak and act with a polluted mind, suffering will follow you, as the wheels of the oxcart follow the footsteps of the ox. Everything is based on mind, is led by mind, is fashioned by mind. If you speak and act with a pure mind, happiness will follow you, as a shadow clings to a form.
—**Buddha**

According to Buddhism as well as metaphysics, our thoughts created the material world, and they continue to influence everything around us, including our "self." This subtle energy, a product of the invisible world, is responsible for our health, our civilization, and our lives. It's much bigger and far more powerful than we can imagine.

Yin-yang energy is what makes everything possible in the universe. It is important to understand that our environment has just as much influence on us as we have on it, and how we respond to our environment can change the course of our lives. We are constantly abiding by the law of cause and effect, which creates existence out of emptiness every day, whether or not we realize it. However, our perception of that existence depends on our level of understanding and awareness.

Science tells us that everything in the universe is made of matter. But did you know that all matter emits energy vibrations at a different speed and frequency? Energy comes from everything, from a single grain of sand to our planet's mightiest creatures, from our own solar system to other galaxies in space. Furthermore, energy comes from our thoughts and emotions, from the simplest idea to great joy or misery. Energy comes from everything humans have ever created.

In their book *The Answer*, John Assarf and Murray Smith write, "Your thoughts not only matter, they create matter. … Thought is where everything comes from." They draw on the theories of quantum physicists Niels Bohr and Werner Heisenberg, who say that "everything in the physical world is made out of atoms. Atoms are made out of energy. And energy is made out of consciousness." They go on to suggest that "everything is energy," elaborating on Albert Einstein's breakthrough theory of relativity: "A rock, a planet, a glass of water, your hand, everything you can touch, taste, or smell—it's all made of molecules, which are made of atoms, which are made of protons and electrons, which are made of nothing but vibrating packets of energy … or packets of possibility." The book in many ways reflects Buddhist philosophy, but it's presented in simple, technical terms that are more credible and comprehensible than the spiritual writings.

As our technology advances to assist our limited, faulty senses, more research supports what Buddhists have believed for thousands of years: that the mind creates all things and that we've hindered ourselves by being trapped by our own egos, our false sense of self.

Medical researchers have been rigorously studying the workings of the human mind, searching for answers to health-related concerns from obesity to ADD to the challenges of prosthetics. In a June 2010 issue in *Popular Science*, Carina Storrs introduces a developing bioengineering technology that would allow paralyzed patients to use their brains to control a robotic prosthetic arm. Developers have learned how to harness mind power and are beginning to flood the market with electronic games and entertainment that use mind-control technology. With its sophisticated understanding of viewers' minds, Hollywood is producing horror movies that are far scarier than they were just a decade or two ago. Is that good or bad? You decide.

Here's a fascinating fact from *The Answer*: During special training, a group of astronauts went for weeks at a time wearing special glasses that allowed them to see the world upside down. Imagine how uncomfortable it must have been for them when everything they saw every day was in an unnatural position. But after weeks of training in the glasses, their brains adjusted and that new perspective looked normal to them.

Another interesting take on how the virtual can become physical is in "Digital Sight for the Blind," an article in the November 2010 issue of *Popular Mechanics*. Writer Jennifer Bogo describes how a group of researchers from the University of Southern California developed a prototype artificial retina that transforms signals from a camera into electrical pulses that stimulate the optic nerve. The technology could give vision to millions who have been suffering from degenerative diseases of the eye.

In "Blind, Yet Seeing: The Brain's Subconscious Visual Sense," published in the *New York Times* in 2008, Benedict Carey describes a fascinating study on blindness conducted by Harvard neuroscientist Beatrice de Gelder and an international team of researchers. The subject of the study was a man who despite being entirely blinded by a stroke was able to see without his eyes. Although the part of his brain that controlled sight was destroyed, Carey wrote, the patient could navigate an obstacle course and "subconsciously" recognize fearful faces. The man at first hesitated to try the obstacle course, Carey writes, but "when he finally tried it … something remarkable happened. He zigzagged down the hall, sidestepping a garbage can, a tripod, a stack of paper and several boxes as if he could see everything clearly." Although the patient was blind, the part of his brain that controlled his ability to sense things in his environment was still functioning normally. It's a function of the sub-cortex, a primitive visual system of the subconscious that we all have.

This shouldn't surprise you—consider animals' extraordinarily keen senses. Bats, for example, use echolocation to navigate in the dark and find their prey, determining every last detail about its size, distance, and motion.

So what's the point of all these findings? It's simple: we see with our brains, not our eyes. The human brain is flexible and can adapt to new circumstances. It has power beyond our imagination, with unlimited capacity for creation. All our modern technologies began as mere ideas. As those researchers studying the human brain discovered, our minds have the vision, focus, and passion to create. Or as Gary Gach wrote, "The true nature of mind is open, transparent, and boundless."

Powers of the Conscious and Subconscious Brain

The true intelligence behind our brain function is phenomenal and worth further exploration. It's fair to say that the human brain is more complex than the world's most complex network systems all put together. The brain is where you hold the seeds of your desire. It's where you develop, mold, and refine your visions. Think of it as the fertile space where all our creations grow. However, it also follows the cosmic law of the universe—the idea that your visions can't come to life unless you take action, and in taking action, you alone bear the liability that may come with it. No one else is to blame but you. If you recognize this truth and follow it, you will be rewarded with the bountiful gifts your heart desires: vibrant health, love, peace, success, and wealth. But if you ignore it, you will become a victim of a failure mentality, which generates all kinds of unfavorable results. When these negative energies start rolling in, it's no wonder terrible things keep pounding you one after another, like raging waves with no end in sight.

Some of us do not realize that our thoughts are the most powerful force in the universe, but it is true. And we can no longer ignore that truth, because it's the basis for establishing our true destiny, for living a meaningful, fulfilled life the way it was meant to be as set forth by cosmic law. Our true nature, or buddha-nature, is happy and joyful, filled with love and compassion. We must reclaim this part of ourselves that's been disconnected from us since birth.

Again I'll refer to *The Answer*, in which John Assarf and Murray Smith discuss the various benefits of understanding the brain's many functions and energies. Those of you who are looking to excel in your business or profession will find this book a real treasure. I'd like to briefly touch on a few important points here.

The brain is small relative to the size of the human body, but as often happens in science and in technology, the smaller something is, the more power it may contain. Assarf and Murray equate the conscious mind to a ship's captain, the decision maker who guides the craft. Although the brain's computing power is far less than that of its partner, the subconscious (a.k.a. the unconscious), it holds an important role in the operation of the ship. This part of the brain is described as the keeper of our imagination and ideas; it uses willpower to make choices, set goals, and evaluate and take risks. It operates in the past and future time frames, but like the RAM in a computer with limited memory capacity, it relies heavily on its partner for other important tasks. The truth is—are you ready for this?—your brain represents only 3–5 percent of your mental power. The rest comes from its partner, the subconscious.

The subconscious brain can be considered the most powerful computer in the universe. If the brain is the ship's captain, the subconscious is the ship's crew, its operating system. Its powers are beyond our comprehension. Its computing power is thousands of times faster than that of the most advanced computer. It records and stores every bit of information about your life from all your senses, and it will feed you only what you're looking for at the time (with or without your knowledge). It is the main engine that keeps everything running smoothly in your body; your body organs and systems all function under its watch. And if you believe in a higher power, it is fair to say that your subconscious is overseen by one of the many spiritual beings of the celestial realm. Furthermore, your intuitive power or instinct—the "all-knowing" part of your faculty—is a vital part of your subconscious.

The Answer describes the subconscious brain as one of the creative marvels of the universe. In computing terms, this part of the brain can process information at speeds of up to four hundred billion bits per second, compared to the conscious brain's speed of only two thousand bits per second. The subconscious operates only in the present—it does not distinguish what's real from what's not, nor does it care. Everything is happening now, in real time, as far as it is concerned. Its memory bank has an unlimited capacity, registering every single moment of our lives for as long as we live.

In short, the subconscious brain is the force behind your every success and achievement. It never loses focus, although the conscious brain is distracted every few seconds. The predominating forces of habit and belief reside in this part of your brain, constantly impacting your life. If you can tap into the subconscious, you'll have unlocked the door to endless possibilities.

So how can you change what's not working in your life? By reprogramming your subconscious so it will have a complete, clear set of instructions for what to do, just like the scripts in a computer that automate its tasks and performances. The goal is to get your subconscious to do as instructed, fulfilling your wishes as commanded.

If you want to change what's not working in your life, the first thing you must do is throw out any old habits and beliefs that have been keeping you stuck. Replace them with newer ones that have higher-frequency vibrations which will benefit you, and reinforce them with new affirmations. After you repeat these affirmations, they will become a habit. Eventually you will do these positive things spontaneously, without thought or effort, the same way you developed your previous, unhealthy habits.

A successful business or profession has three basic components: vision, focus, and action. All successful people share these common characteristics, and you and I can develop them too. Here is how the leading mind works: Our hearts help us establish a vision or purpose in our conscious mind, and our passions help us focus on the prize, assisting us on the path; meanwhile our willpower forces us to take determined action toward our goal. But all this would be meaningless if our subconscious did not create the main motivation to help us reach our final destination. You will find out how to facilitate this process in chapter 5.

Keep in mind that the destructive traits of the ego do not go away. But once you've learned to overcome and conquer the ego, recognizing when it's creeping up on you, your subconscious will reject it. Why? Because you have programmed it to do so.

The Wisdom of Buddha

The name Buddha is given to the supreme divine being Sakyamuni Buddha, who was enlightened more than 2,600 years ago. In Sanskrit, the word *buddha* means "to awaken," or it refers to one who has been awakened. You and I also can be awakened and enlightened if we choose to be. We already have the buddha-nature (the true self, or the soul in Christianity) embedded deep within us. We'll explore that concept in more depth later, but for now we'll just acknowledge that all human beings have this magical gift. The sad thing is, we've been deceived by our five senses, which limit our ability to see beyond our physical world to the real truth. We've been relying only on what we see, hear, smell, taste, and touch.

Here's a classic analogy: Say you've been locked in a room your whole life, and your only view of the outside world comes from peering out a small hole in the wall. That's all you can see, day in and day out. Wouldn't you assume that the world is relatively small? Or think of the Disney film *Tangled*, about the princess Rapunzel, who for eighteen years has lived in a small, high tower deep inside the forest. The woman who keeps her there has lied to her about the outside world. But Rapunzel's heart tells her there's much more to the world than what she sees around her. That's a perfect metaphor for how our eyes and other senses have incapacitated us.

Even with the information available through modern technology, there're still a lot that we don't know.

"I'll believe it when I see it" is a backward statement in my opinion. Imagine if Buddha had told the folks back in his time that they were surrounded by living microorganisms. He wouldn't have been able to convince them, would he? How could he have made people believe what they couldn't see? Won't you agree that the more accurate statement is "Believing is seeing"? Believing is a matter of opening up your mind to see life's many possibilities, not narrowing your world to believe only what you can see. The fact is, you'll never see what you choose not to accept.

As our modern technologies continue to advance, we're gaining a much better understanding of the human brain, and spiritual leaders and metaphysicians around the world are saying we have only scratched the surface of the real truth. We can learn to develop our subconscious and see with intuitive insights; we just have to be willing to open our minds and hearts to do it.

It doesn't matter what you believe about spirituality. Whenever you're in doubt or confused, consider this advice from the Buddha:

"When you know yourselves that these ideas are unprofitable, liable to censure, condemned by the wise, and if they are being adopted and put into effect, they would lead to harm and suffering, then you should abandon them. ... When you know yourselves that these things are wholesome, blameless, commended by the wise, and if they are being adopted and put into effect, they would lead to welfare and happiness, then you should practice them and abide by them."

Chapter 2

Three Reasons Keeping You from Happiness, Good Health, and Success

There is no fire like passion, there is no shark like hatred, there is no snare like folly, there is no torrent like greed.
—**Buddha**

From the emptiness of the universe, humans emerged, and with them the seven emotions: love, hate, desire, fear, joy, grief, and anger. Humans have been trapped under the control of these powers ever since.

Buddha called greed, anger, and ignorance "the three poisons." They are the reasons humans are afflicted with sickness and disease; they are the culprits causing millions of people to lead unhappy lives. They are toxic emotions of the human psyche that take their toll in endless suffering and death. That is why Buddha emphasized their significance in his teaching (dharma), saying, "No enemy can harm one as much as one's own thoughts of craving, thoughts of hate, and thoughts of jealousy." Fortunately, your mind can be as much a medication as a poison, as much your friend as your enemy. The good news is you have total control over the choices you make, and you can choose to overcome any psychological weaknesses that can get you down.

This chapter will begin our emphasis on three key factors in the pursuit of happiness. We will examine the three main causes of unhappiness and why and how they are manifested in human behavior. We will explore different solutions for these conditions, learning how to overcome them

and maintain a healthy mind-set in accordance with the natural laws of the universe. We will also discuss various ways to free yourself from negative thoughts and emotions.

Buddhist texts tie numerous physical illnesses to the obsessive cravings of our five senses. For example, an obsession with physical appearance may lead to liver disease. An excessive attachment to noise may produce kidney disease. Someone who is addicted to aromas may suffer from lung disease, while someone whose habits are driven by the sense of taste may suffer from heart disease, high cholesterol, and diabetes. And one who is too fond of the sensation of touch may suffer from diseases of the spleen.

Now, what I'm about to point out to you may not be pleasant—the truth always hurts. But as you read further, you will find that digging up painful memories or feelings is the beginning step necessary for any real change to occur. We all know that burying your feelings isn't productive; they always find a way to put a dent in your life. Once your suppressed feelings are illuminated by a new understanding of the truth, you'll feel liberated and ready to march through life with a whole new perspective.

Greed

Man, by nature, is never satisfied, and resembles a snake attempting to swallow an elephant; in life, moreover, the praying mantis pounces upon the cicada.
— **Luo Hongxian**

Greed is defined as excessive desire. There's nothing wrong with wanting something, but raging desire can wreak havoc in our lives and those of others. The 2008 global financial crisis, which resulted in a long-lasting recession, was bound to happen in accordance with the principles of the law of cause and effect. Some of us may even call it karma. Since the turn of the new millennium, destructive energies had been gradually evolving from the collective mind-set of greed. The trend toward building quick wealth in real estate and the stock market blinded many investors to the wisdom of making sound investments. Borrowers took on massive, hastily made loans in the short-sighted hope of turning a quick profit. Others took on debt to buy their dream home—a concept that seemed realistic but that really was beyond their capacity. Fraudulent money-making schemes spread rapidly in every corner of the world, from Wall Street to Main Street, until the chase was finally over.

Greed satisfies our momentary desires, but along the way it sets us up for a big fall. How many individuals in the Wall Street scandals have not suffered from their selfish, egotistical acts? Perhaps there are too many to name. What about the greedy government officials—did they all end up in jail? Even if they did escape for now, it's only a matter of time before karma inflicts upon them considerable consequences.

Or consider the same dynamic on a smaller scale—how subconscious emotions can drive us to the edge of insanity. Let's say that you're at a casino, and after a winning streak, feeling luck is on your side, you bet all your hard-earned money on a single hand of blackjack, only to lose it all in the end. Does that sound familiar? There's an old saying that sums it up: "Give him an inch and he'll take a yard." This is greed controlling the better part of you.

Here's a true story from a friend of mine who lost a relative in Vietnam due to the same reason—material attachment. This lady, in her early sixties at the time, had spent twenty years using a small cargo vessel to transport goods from her village in Vietnam to a city across the river. One unfortunate weekend, something caused the ship to go under. Everyone on board was rescued, including her. But although her body was safely ashore, her heart was still clinging to her precious possessions, unwilling to let go. Seeing that the ship was sinking very slowly, she decided to try to save her cargo—and both she and her cargo sank with the ship. Tragic but true.

There are other types of greed that don't involve wealth. Excessive indulgence in food or a craving for power, fame, sex, or drugs often results in habits that are abusive to the mind and body. Think of the last time you couldn't resist gobbling down that last bit of dessert or taking a few more shots of alcohol even though you knew you had reached your limit. Certainly such choices can be devastating blows to your body. Poor eating habits resulting in heart disease are the leading cause of death today, according to the Centers for Disease Control.

The fundamental types of greed are craving, clinging or grasping, and attachment, and each type produces fear, worry, guilt, and false pride. These are the sort of frantic behaviors that keep humans trapped in an endless cycle of suffering, death, and rebirth.

Hatred

When anger rises, think of the consequences.
                                            —Confucius

Hatred, frustration, resentment, and jealousy all are negative emotions that can escalate into uncontrollable anger. When these unhealthy emotional states become chronic, they are the source of peripheral neuropathy, heart attacks, rheumatic disorders, and skin diseases resulting from the constriction of blood vessels. Of Buddha's "three poisons," anger is the most toxic to the mind and body, and it is considered the hardest emotion to overcome or eliminate. When those negative energies that have built up intensify and explode, the results can be devastating to everyone involved. At the very least, anger can hinder the growth of personal relationships—in fact, it's one of the early signs in a failing marriage. As Benjamin Franklin once said, "Whatever is begun in anger ends in shame."

All hateful expressions—whether they are physical, verbal, or just mental—carry equal amounts of negative energy that is potentially dangerous to ourselves and others. Its ripple effects can do far more damage to our loved ones and the world around us than we can imagine.

Just as loving words can brighten up someone's life, hateful remarks can destroy life. Hate is just as deadly as pointing a gun at someone and pulling the trigger—once it's pulled, there's no taking it back. Whether or not the expression of hate was intentional, the relationship of those involved will never be the same; they will always bear deep scars from the experience. Our words can harm and even kill people, and quite often the ones we hurt most besides our loved ones are ourselves. We are the ones who suffer when we experience guilt and regret as a result of our rage. Those negative feelings become harmful energies we store inside, and they can do serious damage to our health in the long run.

We're all too familiar with the nasty things we are capable of doing when we're angry. Fortunately, there's an effective way to eliminate this dangerous emotion: every time you begin to feel angry, stop, recognize that feeling, and then look inside yourself for calming thoughts to soothe your nerves. It's just that simple.

Why do we act the way we do when we know our behavior is damaging? By all means, we must scrutinize our habits to explain the mental process behind them. Hateful rages and unhealthy urges take time to develop into addictions. If we continue our bad habits, the accumulated energies always have negative consequences—sometimes fatal ones.

Ignorance

The learning and knowledge that we have is at the most,
but little compared with that of which we are ignorant.
—Plato

When our hearts and minds are sealed, we shut ourselves out of the process by which new ideas can emerge. We are baffled by our lack of understanding of the true meaning of life, and we become vulnerable to the self-destructive forces of the ego. Anger, fear, and worry creep into our mind at every opportunity until we feel we've lost self-control. We also lose all sense of balance between our regard for self and our regard for others.

There's an old saying that "knowledge is power," which is true—but not completely, in my opinion, because knowledge based on a partial truth is treacherous. It can cause you to dig yourself deeper and deeper into a hole and never see daylight. There is also knowledge without virtue, which is dangerous to the self and the world.

There are many nonbelievers in the world, people who refuse to accept the existence of anything they can't distinguish with their limited senses. If we were to confine ourselves to their ideology, we would have no chance of finding out the real truth about the universe. Humans would have stopped short of inventing new technologies that help our senses delve further into life's endless possibilities. Without believers, our medical advancements would have been severely restricted. What we now know about the human brain has allowed us to solve many of life's mysteries, and we will uncover even more profound truths in the days and years ahead. I think that what we'll discover in the future won't be too far from Buddha's teachings, which already have stood the test of time for thousands of years.

Believing in yourself is important, but believing in a higher level of existence other than your own is even more critical, in my opinion. But even if I were a nonbeliever, I still would choose to follow the principles of a religion. For example, the reason I began learning and following Buddhist philosophy was because it made perfect sense to me—it promotes happiness—and because I felt comfortable with what it had to offer. I do believe that Buddha's teachings have guided and will continue to guide me through difficult times without compromising my own principles. I place images of the Buddha in my home not only as a reminder of what I need to learn from my own ignorance, but also as a sign of respect for him and his teachings, just as I would pay respect to my parents, teachers, or anyone else I admire. Contemplate spiritual wisdom and you shall see riches in your daily life. That's my promise.

Chapter 3

Heal Your Mind, Heal Your Soul

Cures for the Three Poisons

It's known that Buddha was a brilliant doctor; his talks are recorded in the Buddhist sutras. His deep understanding of medicine and science enabled him to heal thousand of diseases. Although he examined patients on both the physical and mental levels, he generally emphasized treatment of the mental state. He believed that greed, hatred, and ignorance breed thousands of sicknesses and diseases. He used the dharma, his teaching, as a prescription. It was his belief that when we're aware of our mental state, we can prevent many serious illnesses from manifesting themselves.

Good feng shui begins here, as well—deep inside our minds and bodies. There is one simple reason why good things don't come easily into our lives: our subconscious mind has blocked them from being actualized. It's only natural for the subconscious to fall back into its comfort zone— that is, to continue to do what it always does, including harboring negative emotions, actions, and reactions that are not to our benefit. The more we desperately seek something (like money, for example), the further away from us it moves. Why? Because our desperation creates pressure inside us, the feeling that we're missing something, and so our subconscious mind simulcasts that negative feeling out to the universe. Fortunately, we can choose not to react that way. We can snap out of this frenetic mind-set by being aware of its existence and setting the intention to correct it.

The preceding chapters cover wisdoms that have been taught by Buddha and other religious leaders for thousands of years. But many prominent individuals naturally possess some of this wisdom without having been taught.

I am certainly hopeful the material in this book is invaluable to you and will help you change your way of life dramatically, as it did for me. Over the past several years, I've taken up the mission to search for the key to happiness. Now don't get me wrong—I am grateful for everything in my life. But like any other human being, I've experienced my share of anguish and discontentment; somehow I always felt dissatisfied in some area of my life. I was deeply troubled by this, and for a few years I simply did not have the answer. For a time I felt money could fill the emptiness in my life, but I learned that I was very wrong. Even though I had a reasonable amount of knowledge about spiritual teachings, the information in my head seemed cluttered and conflicting, scattered like pieces of a puzzle that I couldn't put together. I was totally confused, and at one point I lost faith in the spiritual world entirely.

Fortunately, I still had one unrealized passion that would help free me from those conflicting feelings, from those worries about what was missing in my life. I had a deep love of learning, and I built upon that to overcome the dark emotions that had been jeopardizing the quality of my thoughts. In my search for happiness, I did what I was naturally inclined to do: I conducted more research, digging more deeply into spiritual teachings. Finally I stumbled upon a couple of books that helped clarify the conflicting information in my head. My faith and trust in this search intensified as they mended my heart from its past disappointments. Each new lesson I learned was more exciting than the one before; I realized that one spiritual teacher seemed to fill in what the other ones had missed. What finally helped me break out of my own entrapment for good was the writing of Venerable Master Hsing Yun, from whom I learned about the three poisons. That was the beginning of my transformed view of the meaning of happiness. Then one day in early spring, my entire, frantic search suddenly came to an end. My urge to read more, to keep searching, ceased altogether, and I knew that I had found satisfactory answers to my questions about true happiness. This book was one result. Now I hope it will help you with your own spiritual journey.

Some of the authors (my teachers) mentioned in this book are living spiritual beings, while others may not be. While I've never met any of them personally and don't have any business affiliation with them, their teachings have had a profound impact on my new perspective on the meaning of life. Their insights truly are great contributions to humanity.

At the very least, I hope you'll remember that a healthy mind and body will emit powerful energy that can shield us from harmful external forces while inviting marvelous into our lives. Most of us realize that happiness isn't just about material wealth or physical gratification, but we still don't know what true happiness *is* about. Suffice it to say that when we've taken care of our inner world, our outer world falls into place like magic.

The Power behind Success and Happiness

Finding Yourself

Happiness comes from within. If you choose to be happy, no one and nothing can ever take that happiness from you; success is not found in what you have achieved, but rather in who you have become.
—**Zen Buddhist teaching**

Do you truly accept what's been given to you? Do you feel content with your life? If not, how are you going about changing it? Rebelling against natural law is not the answer; looking inside, to the self, is the right path.

So what is the secret to success and happiness? The answer is incredibly simple: you are! You are your own gatekeeper. You have the power to do what you need to do to be successful and feel content, or you can choose to hold yourself back and feel stuck and depressed. You can also be just as satisfied where you are right now, as opposed to feeling happy only after you've achieved your dreams. When you feel peaceful and full of energy, when you engage in life's activities with passion and a loving attitude, you'll achieve your goals much more easily. You'll also tend to be happier and generally healthier, and certainly not as vulnerable to chronic disease.

I am Buddha!

I'm not being arrogant—it's the truth. You, too, are a buddha, and so is everyone else. You see, according to Buddha, you and I were embodied with a buddha-nature at birth, without even realizing it, and through true wisdom we can rediscover and reconnect with this part of ourselves.

Reclaiming this part of your true nature simply requires looking within. You don't have to travel the world to find truth: delve deep within yourself and you'll find it. I'm reminded of the time I heard my daughters singing along with Hannah Montana's hit song "Find Yourself In You"—and I thought, *That's so true!* (By the way her other hit, "Life's What You Make It," makes a lot of sense too.) Happiness is a choice. How you view your own situation depends on the attitude you choose to have. So let's all join Hannah Montana and "make it rock!"

Novelist George Moore once wrote, "A man travels the world over in search of what he needs, and returns home to find it." Whether we're looking for personal or professional fulfillment, we often look outside ourselves, not realizing that what we're looking for is right under our nose. Then we get frustrated and angry when we can't get what we want; we let our ego slip in, and we start blaming others, judging them when they refuse to come to our rescue.

Contentment is the key to happiness. When the heart is content, life is much easier, and we notice all the delightful things that begin to come before us. Feeling content at every level in our lives removes our inner struggles. Human hearts are like wild horses: they must be tamed before we can enjoy their real beauty up close. We can never see the true beauty inside ourselves if our hearts are running wild all the time. So if we can stop living someone else's life; if we can accept the fact that the grass will always be greener on the other side of the fence and cheerfully enjoy the basic things in life anyway; if we can feel peaceful and not be bothered by the things we don't have; then we will experience the true meaning of life. Likewise, a happy relationship requires love, compassion, trust, and contentment. If either partner in a relationship violates this absolute rule, a breakup is inevitable.

Reducing our desires will help us see our ego for what it is. If we stop grasping at material wealth, we'll free ourselves from the endless cycle of negative emotional drama and eradicate our own greed, one of three root causes of suffering. Perhaps we could contemplate the impurity of qualities like selfishness and blind ambition so that we can lessen our desires. Perhaps we can practice giving away whatever it is we want to receive, doing so with a sincere heart and without expecting anything in return. If we do, the laws of the universe shall reward us in ways we'd never expect—and sometime very generously too.

Life Lessons

If you can't change your fate, change your attitude.

—Albert Einstein

Einstein's quote nails it: nothing is truer, especially when it applies to feng shui practices—the fundamental principles of the art of living. You see, feng shui is considered "man luck," the type of luck that is self-originated, requiring proper thoughts and actions. A simple change in attitude can change the path of your fate. Read on …

Each of us is born into this world with gifts—gifts that are fairly given based upon natural principles. The rewards involved—whether they are manifested in talent, wealth, or power, whether they are inherent or earned—make no difference in the eyes of heaven. What truly matters is how we evolve from there. Our current life is about picking up unfinished business, doing what we ought to have done in the past but didn't, and learning the lessons we failed to learn during this lifetime or previous ones. We must now face those same difficulties once again.

The truth is, we are reborn into the human realm to relearn any incomplete lessons from previous lifetimes—in a way, we're continuing our education. We must evolve as human beings just as everything else in the universe undergoes constant change. As part of our evolution, we must learn to open our hearts, minds, and attitudes in order to adapt, develop, grow, and flow with what life throws at us. Our life lessons, however difficult, are necessary for us to grow spiritually and better ourselves; they help liberate us from our own entrapments. We can work on a personal weakness until we gain a complete understanding about its true nature. In the process we learn why and how things happen to us, and we begin to recognize our own reflection in others' flaws. Until we've evolved, and until we've freed ourselves of all attachments, including the one to self, the universe will continue to set up challenging circumstances for us to experience.

Look around you: everything, including you, conforms to the law of impermanence—what exists today will someday cease to exist. Buddhists believe we are reborn as humans or other beings in this lifetime as the result of our karma. The cycle of our rebirth, suffering, and death will continue for as long as it takes, through numerous lifetimes, until we reach the ultimate enlightened state when our soul no longer needs to come back into this human realm for more lessons. At that point our soul has attained nirvana, the state of eternal bliss. Taoists refer to that state as tao; Christians refer to it as heaven.

We must accept our present life situations as they are, no matter how difficult, and we must have the courage to take full responsibility for our wrongdoings, correct them, and learn from them. Understand that our destiny is right here, right now. Our future (in this lifetime and the next) is happening at this very moment as a result of our deeds and actions. As Alan Kay puts it, "The best way to predict the future is to invent it." You see, destiny is a choice. And with proper thoughts and the right actions, we can create the future the way we envision it—or at least come close to it.

However, our focus should be to free ourselves of desires (cravings) so we can relieve ourselves from attachment (clinging), one of the three poisons. All of us experience crises at some point in our lives, and they aren't a terrible thing if you consider them from a different perspective. When we view a difficult situation through the lens of enlightened wisdom, the situation becomes less critical. Einstein offered this wise advice: "No problems can be solved at the same level of consciousness that created them." When you approach a difficult situation with an intention to resolve it rather than focusing on the problems, you'll see boundless opportunities. In every crisis, there lies an opportunity. There are lessons to be learned indeed if you're willing to change your attitude to see them. Am I implying that accepting a problem will make it magically go away? Of course not. But accepting a tough situation as it is will do three things: First, it will put you in a positive frame of mind to solve your problems. Second, you will no longer be in the position to attract and accumulate more problems. Third, accepting the situation as is will relieve your stress and free you from developing chronic illness.

When you're faced with a dilemma, don't waste your energy on meaningless emotions. Remain calm and at ease, and soon the answer will come to you, whatever is on your mind. Sure, life can be hard. But why make it even harder? You have a choice!

Let's revisit the 2008 global financial crisis. Most of us were affected by the crisis and are still feeling the pain one way or another. Now, I don't mean to be insensitive, but this is an incredible opportunity to learn from our bad experience. Isn't it time to examine ourselves and consider where our wrongful deeds and actions led us? Wouldn't you agree that greed, hatred, and ignorance have everything to do with this world's troubled state of affairs? It seems we'll get closer each day to another world war if we continue on with the current mind-set. Now would be the right moment to eradicate the root cause of unhealthy lifestyles: craving more material wealth. We should settle for what we have and feel satisfied with it. This could be a unique opportunity to be awakened from decades of polluting our hearts through our discontentment. Now is our greatest chance to get in touch with our spiritual side. Don't you think the world would be more peaceful if people focused on love and compassion rather than selfishness and rage?

Let this be one life lesson we don't repeat. Spiritual leaders believe that a substantial number of us have either awakened to the truth or will be awakened to it in the near future. The moment has come for everyone to make the right choices for a better world. As Mahatma Gandhi once said, "You must be the change you wish to see in the world." And may I remind you that the energy of the collective mind-set is far greater than you can imagine? The truth is, we all caused this economy to collapse—and as a whole, we're powerful enough to build a better one. (Later on in this book we will discuss further the universal law of cause and effect and how it applies to everything that exists, including you and me.)

"Great," you might say. "How do I start?" You can start by living your life with the intention of accepting all things and all situations as they are. You can approach problems from a different perspective, accepting the fact that money (and many other factors in life) do not respond to pressure. In fact, the more desperately you want it, the farther it will draw away from you. Don't view your mounting crisis or situation as a struggle you must endure, but as an opportunity from which you can learn. To use an old expression, when life gives you lemons, make lemonade. Decide to be happy even during difficult times. Choosing to feel good about adjusting to your new way of life is the fastest and most meaningful way to recover.

You can start with little things in life like your daily chores, which can be dreadful unless you change your perception to give them meaning. The next time you get stuck in traffic, for example, think of it as a wonderful thing: when your mind is idle, you may have your most brilliant idea or solution to a problem. New ideas are formed when the mind and heart are free from distraction. When your mind is calm it becomes focused, working in the background of your thoughts. At times I've felt alone and a little embarrassed as I water my lawn with outdated technology—a hose—while everyone else in my neighborhood has sprinkler systems. In fact, most of my neighbors have gardeners who take care of their lawns, while I care for mine myself, sweating like a pig. But I'm determined to shut out my ego and stick with the plan for the sake of my health. My new view is that I'm not just getting free exercise, but I'm also getting fresh cosmic energy from the universe, which is vital to my health. Plus, during breaks from my labors, I enjoy the serenity in the company of nature, which allows me to release stress and replenish my chi.

You can start by living your life right now, in the present moment, and not letting hurtful memories bog you down. Stop worrying about the future, for your future is in whatever you're doing now. The Bible says a man reaps what he sows—and that's very true indeed. You'll get whatever you're planting right now. So begin by communicating love and compassion to those around you; express loving thoughts to people you meet and greet daily. Try this for a week or two, and I promise you'll notice something inside you begin to change. Your new view of the outer world will be more colorful than the old one because it comes from your true nature, not from your ego. Contemplate this Taoist saying: "The whole world can see the beautiful as the beautiful only because of the ugly. The whole world can recognize the good as the good only because of the bad. Something and nothing create each other. The difficult and the easy complement each other." We can truly appreciate joy only because we have experienced sorrow. We see abundant stars only in the darkest part of the sky. It is all about your perception of the world.

Perhaps one of the least obvious ways to learn about true living is by taking a closer look at death. An intriguing book about other realms or planes of existence is *The Tibetan Book of the Dead* by Francesca Fremante and Chögyam Trungpa, who discuss the soul's journey after death. In Buddhism, as opposed to other religions, it is stated that we are ultimately judged not by God, Buddha, or any other supreme being, but by our own karmic deeds and conduct. After we've departed the human realm, what we were and experienced during our living days will carry on beyond the grave. What we leave behind are our physical possessions and our loved ones. Only our spirits or consciousness will live on forever, moving from one form into another and from one realm to another.

Upon death, our soul remains to enter into a different state of existence. What it experiences on the journey to reincarnation will be determined by our characteristics or our state of mind. Immediately after death and before reincarnation, the soul enters the bardo, an intermediate state where it experiences joy or suffering depending on the good or bad karma it accumulated during the past life. It will continue that cycle over and over until the final state of reincarnation takes place and the soul enters any one of six realms of existence: sainthood, heaven, human, ghost, animal, or hell. This reincarnation may or may not be in the form of a human being; it could be in the form of an animal, an insect, or even another being entirely. Only an enlightened soul is believed not to have to be reborn. It has liberated itself from the cycle of rebirth, suffering, and death, and it shall remain in eternal bliss in the pure land. It's considered to be in union with heaven.

While *The Tibetan Book of the Dead* focuses on liberating a dying person at the time of death, it is crucial that we retain a positive frame of mind at all times. Our attitude now sets the stage for where we go and what we become after we die. In order to live in harmony with the principles of cosmic law, we must have a keen understanding of life. We must face, accept, and learn from life's challenging lessons over the course of our entire lives, because if we don't, we will face them over and over again—in this lifetime, after death, and in the next life, until the chain is broken and dissolved through self-realization. There's no easy way out. For example, in Buddhist philosophy, someone who commits suicide is thought to have not fully understood life's lessons; hence he or she will come back as a human being only to face the same challenges again. The shipwreck story is another example of someone who did not learn to let go of extreme attachments and so was destined to return to the human realm for another trial.

Fate brings you together with those around you. The people and events that we find challenging represent problems we must resolve by changing ourselves, not others, for those challenges are only reflections of us. Quite often we are placed in situations of conflict, and we need to learn from the people around us. If someone in your life always quarrels with you and makes you feel miserable, perhaps you should look for love within yourself. A lack of love inside you is likely the main cause of your depression, and feeling angry and resentful toward the other person (which is really toward yourself) won't solve anything. No matter how difficult the situation gets, embrace it as a lesson to be learned in this lifetime. Understand that you and the other person share the same pain, and that a head-to-head conflict will only intensify the situation. When you initiate kindness and express compassion for the other person without any expectations in return, your love and patience will soften the other person's heart just as the warm sun melts ice.

Sure, we can't rid ourselves of all our toxic emotions and learn everything in a single lifetime—and we shouldn't feel despair that we can't. But we should do our best to eradicate as much negativity as we possibly can. The sooner we learn from and correct those harmful mistakes and wrong deeds, the better our lives will be in the immediate future. But it's most promising to look forward to our next several lives, because each new life, when lived properly, will surpass the preceding one as set forth by the cosmic laws of heaven.

That said, life lessons are very difficult ones, and there aren't any shortcuts we can take to avoid them. Passing those life lesson exams is the one and only way to liberate ourselves from the "Wheel of Life."

The secrets to living according to the natural laws of the universe are as described in the dharma: contemplate and eradicate the three poisons, and open your heart and mind to spiritual wisdom for continuous growth. If you can follow Buddha's Eight Paths, you will be free. In short, if you truly understand the laws of impermanence, you will find contentment and real happiness in your life. Where you obtain spiritual wisdom does not matter, although ideally, you do not need guidance from any religious group or organization, because liberation comes entirely from within.

Meditation and faithful prayer are two daily practices we can use to cultivate our well-being. Meditation, according to Tao, is "the art of listening," and it is by all means beneficial to our physical and mental health. Through daily meditation you can generate a healthy aura that is naturally vibrant—your energy field will constantly interact with the energy flows of the universe. For that reason alone, meditation can be an excellent starting point for making change in your life, but there are many more benefits too. First and foremost, meditation can help prevent the development of chronic disease caused by living in a stressful environment. Meditation calms your mind, heals your body, helps you relax, clears your thinking, raises your wisdom, and strengthens your ability to concentrate—there are too many benefits *not* to practice it. We will talk about various methods of meditation later on, in chapter 5. Meanwhile, if you want to explore the subject further, check out *The Complete Idiot's Guide to Buddhism* by Gary Gach. Don't be off-put by the title: Gach does a great job of explaining how to see life from a new, higher perspective and live life according to Buddhism's "Middle Way."

Eradicating Toxic Emotions

Rise above Ignorance

As hunger is cured by food, so ignorance is cured by study.
—**Chinese proverb**

When we're ignorant, we've committed ourselves to a poor quality of life, one in which we're unable to understand or see beyond the situations in which we find ourselves. We refuse to accept reality for what it is; hence we continue to struggle against it. Our lack of knowledge generates fear and worry, and our anger and denial can dampen and perhaps prolong the healing process. Blaming other people for our own misery is a common expression of denial whose negative effects are exponential.

Above all, we should recognize and learn from these detrimental emotions so we can prepare ourselves for life's one inevitability: loss. If you've ever contemplated the law of impermanence, you understand that loss is as natural as it can be. In fact, nature can teach us a great deal about impermanence. Loss occurs in both the tangible and the intangible worlds; it's only a matter of time. What I want to point out here is that wisdom can help us cope with the loss of our possessions, our loved ones or their health, or our own health.

Wisdom is the best cure for ignorance. To prepare yourself for loss, contemplate the laws of cause and effect and impermanence to rid yourself of attachments. Take note of the fact that most wise people aren't necessary wealthy, yet their happiness surpasses that of wealthy people. Their riches lie in their inner peace. They understand the natural order of the universe and the pain that comes with attachment. What they pursue is beyond material wealth; eternal bliss cannot be found in the human dimension.

Subdue Hatred and Overcome Anger

Holding on to anger is like grasping a hot coal with the intent of throwing it at someone else; you are the one who gets burned.
—**Buddha**

Anger and hatred poison the heart and cause poor circulation in the body. These emotions may be the most overlooked cause of heart problems. In fact, medical research seems to agree with religious theory here. When an individual is angry, unhappy, or under pressure, the person is said to be in a state of chemical imbalance: that's when the brain releases adrenalin and noradrenalin, which can act as toxins to the brain and body and can block healing. Essentially, these chemicals can weaken the physical body while disrupting the mind. They can reduce the immune system's ability to combat diseases, and they can obscure our thinking, which can contribute stress and lead to serious depression. If we reach such a state, we lose interest in doing anything and eventually lose pleasure in life. These prolonged emotional conditions may be linked to digestive disorders and heart attacks.

When you're holding a grudge against someone, who do you think is suffering? It's you, of course. Your enemy likely has moved on with his or her life while you're still wracked with resentment. These unresolved feelings will only get more deeply embedded in your subconscious mind, and that is not in your best interest. In fact, it will only make you a bitter person, causing all the people around you to distance themselves. The Dalai Lama once said, "We can never obtain peace in the outer world until we make peace with ourselves." That is so true. How can we achieve world peace while frustration and anger boil inside us?

We're all aware of the alarming rise in bullying in schools and in cyberspace; it's a problem we all should take seriously. The fact is, bullying exists in our society at all levels: among family members, among coworkers, and even among nations. There are three common qualities bullies share: anger, the desire for power, and a need for attention. At a deeper level, bullies aren't necessarily angry at their victims; bullies are angry about their own lives and vent their repressed anger by victimizing someone else. Bullying gives them a sense of power and place in society—but it's a false perception created by the ego. The truth is, the bully is weak and vulnerable on the inside; hence the need to cover up this truth. The desire for love and attention may be the bully's underlying motivation. It's much easier to confront bullies when we understand where they're coming from. Then we can help them see that their behavior harms themselves as well as their victims, and it certainly doesn't fill what's missing in their lives.

You could say that bullies' egos have taken over their lives, and it is our duty as humans to help them recognize that their behavior is wrong. Without proper guidance to awaken their true nature, they will continue that behavior, posing a threat to others and themselves.

Tolerance is one way to combat anger and hatred, but being firm at the same time is the key to ensuring that things don't get out of control. Being tolerant in your daily dealings with others helps rid your life of unnecessary frustration. And practicing kindness and compassion in your personal and professional lives will elevate your energy vibrations to a higher level, where they will flow harmoniously with the universal energy source. Your health will be the biggest beneficiary of your new attitude.

Fear and Worry

> *Fear always springs from ignorance.*
> —**Ralph Waldo Emerson**

One of the most common causes of failure and unhappiness is fear, which affects your actions and your decision-making capability. Fear is often disguised by your ego to keep you feeling stuck, worried, and stressed. Generally, it is a fear of losing what you already have, whether it's your career, your money, your health, or a relationship. In other words, your attachments are making you worried sick. Because of your fear you may feel hopeless or even try to escape from the world—but that won't help, either. Because fear is such a strong, destructive emotion, it falls under one of the three poisons in Buddhism. According to the tenets of Chinese medicine, extreme fear can do serious damage to the heart, kidney, and bladder, while excessive worry injures the stomach and spleen.

Chronic illnesses like neurological diseases or chronic conditions like peripheral neuropathy can generate fears and worries and certainly increase our stress. Most of us have either experienced such symptoms ourselves or know someone who has. However, we can eliminate or reduce those harmful emotions if we are willing to educate ourselves about our physical condition and take part in the healing process with the help of doctors and therapists.

Fear and worry come in many forms. Most are self-generated, but some come from Mother Nature, like Hurricane Katrina in August 2005 and the shocking disaster that hit Japan on March 11, 2011, when a 9.0-magnitude earthquake caused a tsunami that engulfed the country's eastern coastline. That terrifying event left permanent scars on the psyches of the Japanese people. Incidents like these generate tremendous fears and worries—the greatest of which is not knowing what to expect next.

It's only human to be afraid of what we don't know or understand. In fact, sometimes we try to escape our fears by ignoring them altogether—that's especially true with young children. Perhaps fears and worries have prevented you from making life-changing decisions or pursuing your dreams. Well, those fears and worries are coming from your ego, your false self. That's the little voice inside your head telling you that you're not good enough to do this or that or saying, *You don't know what you're getting into.* Because of this, we often don't follow through with actions that would be the cornerstone to building our dreams. We are too afraid to get out of our comfort zone, because that would require losing the things our ego is clinging to. But the greater loss is the thing your fear keeps you from doing.

So the next time you catch yourself fantasizing about your dreams and frightened about all the work and difficulty it would take to achieve them, stop and think of Henry Ford's encouraging advice that "obstacles are those frightful things you see when you take your eyes off your goal" and "whether you think you can, or that you can't, you are usually right." It's that simple.

What else can you do to overcome your fears? Get out of your comfort zone and follow through with decisive action. And here's another proven method for facing fear, from rocket scientist Wernher Von Braun: "Research is what I'm doing when I don't know what I'm doing." We fear what we don't know, and the best way to overcome that fear is educate ourselves. Besides books and videos, we have at our disposal a world of information waiting for us on the Internet—it is the search engine outside of our brains.

Fear is a state of mind subject to control and direction by our conscious mind. We've all been given a wonderful gift: absolute control over our thoughts. When we choose to think negative thoughts, we will be filled with fears and worries; when we choose to think positive thoughts, they will give birth to new ideas, safeguarding our dreams.

> *The illusion of limitation—with its fear and sense of frustration—is born of the false perception that the only resource available to you in the moment of challenge is what you already know as being possible for you to do.*
> **—Guy Finley**

Fear is a natural response of self-preservation in difficult situations. It's our way of staying out of harm's way. But irrational fear can obscure our thinking; it stirs up other emotions that hamper our ability to see our situation clearly when it comes to making decisions. In *Life's Missing*

Instruction Manual, author Joe Vitale shares Cindy Cashman's three keys for handling fears and maintaining a clear perspective: "Ask, Answer, and Action."

Cashman recommends asking yourself quality questions that begin with *what* instead of *why*—like *What is stopping me from getting what I want?* This kind of introspective question forces your higher self to get to the root cause of your problem. On the other hand, a self-destructive question might be *Why do bad things always happen to me?* Such questions perpetuate negativity by validating suppressed emotions like self-pity, jealousy, anger, blame, and resentment. Such unhealthy emotions are really pockets of resistance keeping you stuck at your current life level and preventing access to your true self (buddha-nature).

Cashman says that honestly answering these types of questions can give you a whole new perspective on your situation. It forces you to examine and acknowledge your emotional state; in doing so, it breaks up pockets of resistance within you and helps kick-start the process of receiving spiritual insight.

Cashman also names two important steps that comprise Action: Adopt and Allow. Let's take a moment to explore these two steps that can liberate you from your false self (ego), which can drive you to insanity at times. These steps can free you from the madness of daily life as you deal with family members, friends, finances, work, school, and so on.

Acceptance and Letting Go

> *There are only two tragedies in life: one is not getting what one wants, and the other is getting it.*
> —Oscar Wilde

Cashman's advice to Adopt and Allow can be explained this way: Adopting is acceptance, and Allowing means letting go. Acceptance breaks apart the negative energies that have bonded within you, easing your inner struggles, and letting go releases those energies to allow room for new, positive ones to emerge.

When you truly accept difficult situations as they are, you're essentially removing the inner conflict between your reality and your desire for happiness and contentment. This is the simplest but most important step you can take to make a change in your life. Once that happens, serenity will naturally set in to replace your negative emotions. Then, when your heart is calm and your mind is clear, you'll see the light of many possibilities. You'll have taken the necessary first step to unblocking your path to liberation. That may seem like an impossible thing to do, but it may be your only choice. Remember the shipwreck story? We should learn from it for the sake of our souls. Letting go of our loss is inarguably a torturous feeling, but it's nothing compared to losing our lives.

Two emotions worth mentioning here are pride and self-pity. Right now you may be letting pride stand in the way of resolving a conflict between you and a loved one. The magnitude of pride's destructive power is inconceivable; we can see it in relationships at home and in the workplace and even at sporting events, and someone always ends up getting hurt along the way. If we can truly see how fragile life is, then we can behave with compassion and mindful awareness of our conduct, knowing that each action we take has consequences. We then won't unintentionally add emotional fuel to an already fragile situation. I know that letting go of our pride is easier said than done, but think of the impact it will have if we don't; our happiness, and the happiness of everyone around us, depends on this selfless act of letting go. Really, it's the only way to rid ourselves of grudges that we've been holding into for so long. For the sake of our own spirit, now is the time to swallow our pride and let the healing begin, bringing peace and serenity back into our lives—for our own benefit and that of our loved ones.

Self-pity is form of suffering generated by self-delusion—a product of the false self (ego). Many people give up hope at some point because of self-pity, whether the problem involves money, career, or a relationship. Self-pity never results in anything good. We see its devastating results in teens, who have become increasingly vulnerable in our high-stress society because they're young and ill-equipped to cope in a harsh environment. Unfortunately, some teens who feel trapped and can't see a way out of their distress resort to taking their own lives as a way of ending their problems.

Self-pity can be our greatest enemy, keeping us in a constant battle with ourselves. The ego's agenda is to make us feel fearful and sorry for ourselves. If we can recognize that the ego thrives on our weakness, we can wisely refuse to give in, becoming even stronger than our ego in the process. We can adjust our view of our situation, adapting a new attitude to do the right thing—to see our failures as opportunities to learn valuable lessons in this lifetime for the sake of our well-being. We certainly have the option of seeking professional help, providing we admit that we can't combat our problems alone. And we can always turn to spiritual guidance during our darkest hours. One thing to keep in mind is that however severe our problems seem now, they will pass, as they always do.

Forgiveness is an excellent way to subdue your own anger. When you remove the anger within, your resentment toward someone or your situation will gradually dissolve; you'll weaken its power until it has no relevance to your new state of mind. Furthermore, releasing those old, unhealthy energies prevents buildup that can clog your thinking, possibly helping you avoid depression altogether. Forgiving someone is actually forgiving yourself—you generate the intention of removing the pain inside you, you prepare yourself for healing, and, as the old saying goes, "Time heals all wounds." In time those angry feelings will cease, leaving an empty space to be filled with something joyful.

Unresolved issues serve only to repress the emotions. It is not unusual for symptoms to lie dormant only to surface two or three years after a traumatic event. Painful events like a loss or a big fight usually end in trapped, lingering feelings. The good news is that we can speed up the healing process if we understand the cause of our trapped feelings and know how to remove them completely.

Once you have conquered pride and self-pity, you and everyone around you will benefit from your new outlook. First of all, your greatest enemy, yourself, now has become your ally. That means you will no longer be engaged in constant internal battle. You also will have learned many things from this former enemy that you never knew before: you're now more tolerant of others' misbehavior and more understanding about their hardships, as you can relate them to your own. This new mind-set will only grow stronger when you develop other, higher-energy feelings like love and compassion.

As Oscar Wilde suggested, getting what you want isn't necessary a good thing—especially if it results in negative consequences. For example, we've all seen the high price people pay as the result of their own misconduct in the workplace, in politics, in religion, etc. Families are torn apart, friendships end, and careers are ruined for just a few moments of excitement. Were they really worth it? We are constantly bombarded with temptations as we interact with others—from media exposure to the world of the Internet. The truth is, the untamed heart is a dangerous thing that can tarnish your reputation or ruin your life at any time. We must keep it under control by being mindfully aware of the choices we make, asking ourselves, *What are the possible consequences if I make that choice?* and *Will I hurt anyone with this behavior, including myself?*

Questions like these prompt us to pause briefly and allow our consciousness to regain control of our thoughts—enabling us to make better judgments when we are most vulnerable, especially when we're under pressure and definitely not at our best.

All emotions are natural human conditions; they are the cause of all human suffering. While nothing in the world can change that, what we can do is be mindful of our condition, accept it, adapt, and move on. The more we do so, the more happy, peaceful, successful, and loving we will become.

Our ego thrives on our negative emotions; unless we can see the ego for what it is, it will keep us apart from our true nature for as long as we allow it to deceive us. Not only will it bring us poor health, but it will prevent happiness from coming into our lives.

Confession and Prayer

Confession is another way to release negative energies that are stored inside you, and it is an effective psychological approach for releasing emotional strain. Confess to anyone, especially God or the Supreme Being; by confessing, you're alleviating the mental burden of impure thoughts like fear, worry, anger, guilt, and resentment. These emotions are toxic, the culprits behind illness and disease and obstacles to your future success and dreams.

It doesn't matter what religion you believe in; what matters is the fact that prayer does heal. The power of prayer is directly linked to the unconscious mind. When you're praying with a sincere heart, you're essentially creating the right mental picture of your condition, along with the powers to release it. The heavens are always listening and always ready to give to those who ask. One key to unlocking that rigid side of yours is to believe without doubt: trust that you will receive. That's just one more way to remove the inner blockages that may have prevented many delightful things from coming into your life.

Chapter 4

The Power of Transformation

The Present Is All That Matters

Do not dwell in the past, do not dream of the future,
concentrate the mind on the present moment.
—Buddha

When we live in the past and worry about the future, we make ourselves vulnerable to poor health. We build up so many emotions about the destination that we forget about the journey itself. But the truth is, the journey is just as important, if not more so, because whatever we do or feel during the journey will determine its outcome—the destination. Consider the example of parents who spend all their time working, building up wealth in order to secure their children's future years down the road. Though it's a viable plan, it's not always sustainable. What these parents don't realize is they're losing a lot while they are away from their children. Their busy schedules don't allow them time or energy to cherish the everyday moments with their children until it's too late—either the children outgrow the bonding moment or some unfortunate incident occurs to keep parents and children apart.

Meanwhile, these overworked parents come home exhausted, perhaps bringing home their unpleasant mood from work. They pay little or no attention to the children while generating an unhealthy environment in the home. Meanwhile their health begins declining from prolonged stress and tension at work.

We often forget that children don't look to the future for their happiness. All they know is that their mommy or daddy is not there during those moments to share their feelings. Those may be the most important moments for them, the ones that will have the greatest impact in their lives, and their parents are missing out.

This scenario illustrates how someone with a loving and caring intention can carry it out with an unmindful, unbalanced approach. It's a good idea to examine our thoughts and actions from time to time to ensure our approach is best for everyone involved and is not just for the sake of the future, which offers no guarantees.

The ancient Taoists offered this wisdom: "The past is over. The future will never come. Now is the only moment that will ever exist. Therefore, live each moment to the fullest." Only the *present* is real, folks. That's where ideas are being born and creations are taking shape. It's where real potential is revealed in this fertile emptiness. The present is the moment in which our inner space rises and expands; it offers our only access to spiritual insight. The past is great, but it's only for our reference. Every present moment dictates the future, which will then become the present, too, when it gets here. Certainly a properly planned future is important; it contains the promise of our hopes and dreams. But we must not become enslaved by it, allowing it to throw us off balance in other areas of our lives.

Emptiness: A Boundless Void

Prosperity is not in what you have attained, but rather in what you give away ... for it is only when you become empty that you can be filled with something greater.
—Zen Buddhist saying

Emptiness is nondependent, impermanent, unattached, and without tangible entity, as defined by Gary Gach. It is a space unbounded by time, in which everything is possible—or as Gach puts it, "a realm of limitless possibility." Impermanence is not a bad thing, he notes: "[It] allows events to keep coming.

Impermanence implies that the formation that exists now will one day cease and revert to its origination in emptiness. Thus we live in constantly changing circumstances, and we can see this phenomenon in everything around us: the aging of the stars and planets, the cycle of life on earth, our seasons and climates, and so on.

This state can be understood in the Buddhist saying "Form is emptiness; emptiness is form." The vast, empty space of the universe was a womb that gave birth to our planets, stars, and galaxies; hence we called it the universe. Without emptiness, there would be no space for a universe, and without everything that exists in the universe, there would be no empty space. Gach boils that concept down to Einstein's theory of relativity, $E = mc^2$, which shows that energy becomes matter, and matter becomes energy. We can also refer to the yin-yang principle of balance: everything is interdependent, everything necessarily coexists with something else, with each existing only because of the other (such as with the past, present, and future). This concept also coincides with Buddha's doctrine of emptiness, which states that emptiness is a phenomenon with no beginning or end, that emptiness causes something else to exist, and that this existence can be perceived only through emptiness.

Emptiness does not necessary mean "nothingness"—you don't have to bankrupt yourself to get something greater. I like to think of it as having a glass half-full, where there is always room for something new and better. If I want wisdom, I must have an open mind and an attitude that fosters learning, not ignorance. Likewise, if I want a loving, intimate relationship with my wife, I must return the love I receive from her, leaving some room inside me to be filled. If I give back love and attention without any expectations in return, in due time, when the conditions have ripened, the law of cause and effect will ensure I am rewarded for my efforts.

There is one fascinating thing about this void of space we call emptiness: it is where our creations are born and our ideas are disseminated. All human inventions and creative work were once only ideas, products of our fertile imagination, the vast empty space in our mind. In the chapter ahead, we will explore different meditation techniques to help us get into this fertile state of mind.

There are many books and videos that cover this subject; perhaps the most popular is the *The Law of Attraction*, about the boundless void of space in our mind, which is immensely powerful once we invoke and recognize it. You can apply the book's principles in all areas of your life for self-advancement and to help others around you understand this truth.

The Aura: Your Personal Energy Field and Radar

Your aura is the energy field your body emits in the form of light, electricity, heat, electromagnetism, and other types of energy. It's a sensory measure of your mind and body's well-being prior to birth and throughout your lifetime. It is your life force, or chi, surrounding your body, constantly broadcasting to the universe your thoughts, desires, and physical condition. It's the reason we can sense each other's feelings, just as we can feel the bad vibes in a room or from a person. Some people can literally see the colors of the aura surrounding a person or animal or even a tree. You can see aura depicted as a halo in early images of holy saints in different religions.

The aura is also a form of protection shielding you from outside negative forces (bad luck). Your aura became distorted and weak when you are sick, distressed, depressed, angry, or intoxicated. Under such conditions you're more easily impacted by external negative forces and therefore likely to attract more of what you don't want. But when you feel well—peaceful, happy, faithful, and joyful—your aura glows and expands, generating a variety of vibrant energies that match those in the higher levels of the universe. You'll be able to tap into those other realms for help and guidance much more easily.

There are seven realms of existence that humans normally can't see, according to Ted Andrews in his book, *How to Meet and Work with Spirit Guides*. Our perception usually limits our ability to see these invisible energy fields, he says, but there are ways that we can use meditation to reconnect with this part of ourselves. For an in-depth look at how you can learn to see and improve your energy fields, read Andrews's other book, *How to Read and See the Aura*. It's unfortunate that most people don't know about the energy fields that exist in and around us all the time. But now that you do, keep an open mind and try to recognize their existence. It certainly would be to your benefit.

Intuition: Your Own Spiritual Guide

Follow your instincts. That's where true wisdom manifests itself.
—Oprah Winfrey

Whenever you get caught "between the devil and the deep blue sea," don't ask the devil—your ego—for advice. Instead, go to your intuition for guidance. That's where the light always shines brightest. Let the intuitive sense speak to you with clarity to help you resolve internal conflicts resulting from your current life situations. This spiritual part of you, the unseen intelligence, is always right, and it always vibrates at a high energy level, linking you to the universal source. Trust it and you will get your answers and overcome your fears.

In order for good things to come into your life, you must be your highest, truest self when you make important decisions, and you should train your subconscious to alert you whenever the conditions for good luck are right so you'll be at the right place at the right time. You'll also need guidance from superior powers to show you where to go, whom to meet, and what to do to fulfill your requests or desires.

One way is to invoke that all-knowing part of yourself, your own spiritual guide, your intuition. It is the part that is smart, wise, tuned in to nature—a gateway connecting you with the universal source and supreme beings. Intuition is not the ego, and it has no form. "It operates beyond time and space; it is a link to your higher self," explains Sanaya Roman in her book *Personal Power through Awareness*. "It operates knowing that past, present, and future are simultaneous," adding that "it speaks to you through insights, revelations, and urges." Buddhists refer to intuition as the wisdom eye." Others refer to it as "gut feelings" or "the sixth sense."

The intuitive guide works in the conjoined space of emptiness I mentioned earlier: your subconscious, in which ideas, events, people, and resources are formed. The law of cause and effect is constantly at work here, responding to our every thought and effort. To use a simple analogy, it works the same way as an Internet search engine: our intentions and thoughts are like key search terms we send out into cyberspace, knowing it will return the results to us. Our intuition, a reputable search engine, gathers information from the universe and brings it to our attention while filtering out everything that may be irrelevant to our search.

Our intuition feeds us bits of information at a time without warning, so we must be mindfully aware of them when they come to us. The information can be in the form of symbols, phrases, words, numbers, people, or things, and they can appear in our waking lives or in our dreams. If we want to know what a certain dream means, a dream dictionary can help us decode these mysterious signs and messages from our intuition.

You know you're being guided by your intuition when you have a gut feeling, insight, or sudden urge to do something specific that doesn't necessarily make sense or follow any order or logic. Intuition always talks to you in the present, subtly but sometimes forcefully, too, to get your attention. When you suddenly just know what to do, that's your intuition speaking to you. When you stay focused at this level, your thoughts become clearer and good things can come into your life a lot more easily. For intuition to work most powerfully, it's imperative that you do two things: act and trust.

Acting on that sudden urge before the intellectual or logical part of your ego kicks in is the real key here. Why? Because once your logic takes over and starts analyzing the situation, you've lost it. When you act on intuition, trust it whole-heartedly. Trust the messages that come to you. Again, if there's any part of you that doubts, you've lost it. Maintain that tuned-in state so that your intuition remains accessible, always ready at the highest level each time it's called to help. I should note that the above-mentioned "urge" is not used in the same context as the urge to eat, for example. This urge is generated from a healthy and proper state of mind.

I have had a variety of experiences when I've taken action with intuition as my guide, from little incidents to life-changing events. There were also many instances in the past when I used intuition in a practical way in my education and career. At the time I didn't entirely understand how I accomplished all that I did, with miraculous results. Now when I look back at each of those experiences, I realize they had something in common: in each case I had intention, focus, action, and hope, the basic building blocks of intuition to help you achieve your goals. I know some of you may have had similar experiences—but if you haven't, it may be it time to ask your intuition for guidance.

Following your intuition will lead you to ample opportunities as you break through layers of resistance in all areas of your life. You'll develop a strong ability to *know*, letting your intuition speak to you and guide you. Listen with a silent mind. When you're relaxed, when you're quietly paying attention, you will do the right thing.

Intuition requires intention, focus, trust, and a determination to bring its power forward so that your desires can be made manifest. The Tao says that following our intuition is "the Way" to joyful living, and that intuition can help us live according to the natural laws of the universe. Sanaya Roman says, "Acting on intuition brings your goals to you faster." So act with confidence. Place your unquestioning trust in what your instinct is telling you to do, because its nature is always right, always in harmony with the energy flows of the universe.

The Power of Prayer

Ask, and it shall be given to you, seek, and you will
find, knock, and it shall be opened to you.
—(Matthew 7:7)

Believe and miracles will happen. Prayer is about speaking your mind. Praying mindfully can put you in a mental state that allows you direct contact with superior beings so you can receive guidance from the higher realms of existence—invoking your intuition, giving you hope, and bringing faith into your life. Praying with a sincere heart and focusing with positive intention can produce high-energy vibrations that penetrate deep into the mind and body for healing and transformation. Believe without a doubt that your prayer will be answered, because doubt creates resistance to receiving that answer. That said, praying without positive action guided by intuition is like expecting heaven to drop food into your open hands. It's not going to happen, no matter who your god is. Heaven helps those who help themselves.

Prayer broadcasts your energies out into the universe, where the law of cause and effect will accommodate your request. You might ask, "What happens if I unintentionally broadcast negative energies such as fear, anger, or hate?" Whether it's intended or not, you'll get back what the universe received from your energy. Remember the old saying "Be careful what you wish for"? That explains this principle exactly. The universe will always let you experience more of whatever you broadcast; it never stops responding to your requests. Its nature is to complement and deliver what's been asked for.

Earlier I briefly mentioned the power of thought, and I would add that you cannot simultaneously project two opposing thoughts—one will eventually overpower the other. For example, if you're feeling happy at this very moment, you cannot possibly be thinking angry or sad thoughts—and vice versa. You cannot hate when your heart is filled with warmth and compassion. Knowing this rule can be very helpful when you're dealing with emotions; it requires power to overcome the ego.

The truth is, when we meditate with intention, we can maintain a peaceful and happy state of mind whenever we feel we're drifting off course. Daily meditation is a powerful way to invoke happy thoughts and feelings. The power of prayer can also put us in that positive mental condition and keep it afloat.

Reciting a mantra or words that have spiritual meaning is a strong start; it will set the right tone, suggesting a reason for making changes in your life, and it's extremely effective during a meditative state. For example, whenever I feel frightened or confused, I repeat the mantra of Bodhisattva Guan Yin: *Namo Guan Shi yin Pusa*. It is one of the ways I call upon her for guidance.

For those who don't know of her, Guan Shi Yin (or *Avalokieshvara*, in Sanskrit) is known as the one "who perceives the sounds of the world." She is the goddess of mercy, who vowed not to rest until all sentient beings were free from the cycle of rebirth. It was recorded in the sacred Buddhist texts that before she reached sainthood, she had more than 350 incarnations along her path to liberate the people from suffering. She assumed a multitude of manifestations, including male and female forms. Her long and fascinating history dates as far back as AD 200. Her divine spirit still resonates loudly in the hearts of millions of people in all parts of the world. Ask for her help and guidance during difficult times. To learn more about her, read the book by Martin Palmer, Jay Ramsay, and Man-Ho Kwok, *The Kuan Yin Chronicles: The Myths and Prophecies of the Chinese Goddess of Compassion*. Getting to know her may become a blessing in your life.

Love and Compassion

If you've been feeling sad lately, a lack of love may be to blame. Perhaps you've heard that "love makes the world go 'round." There's nothing truer than that simple phrase. Love is the essence of life, the life-giving spirit of our heart, the universal life force of our existence; it is "the Way" as suggested by Tao. Compassion is an expression of the true meaning of love. You can tell people you love them, but if you don't show compassion, your words are just that, without real meaning. Try this simple act in your daily life: greet and treat everyone with compassion, and I can assure you that the gestures of affection you'll get in return will be enormous.

And what is unconditional love? It goes beyond lending someone a helping hand; it is tolerating others' misbehavior while providing guidance to help them recognize their own misconduct. For example, helping someone out of a bad situation with money alone is not unconditional love because the root cause of the mistake has not been addressed, so the person is likely to repeat the same mistake again and again. Lao Tzu, the father of Taoism, once said, "Give a man a fish, feed him for a day. Teach a man to fish, feed him for life." This ancient wisdom deserves to be embraced and put into practice. Expressing unconditional love for yourself and others is the greatest medicine for anger and hatred. A healthy balance of body and mind is critical to your success and happiness, and it begins with a simple act of kindness.

Practice Patience

Our society has gotten to a point where our patience has been lost to the whim of technological advancement. We have developed and indeed encouraged in future generations the expectation of instant gratification. Everything we could ever want to satisfy our sensual pleasures we can get instantly with some help from electronic gadgets. We have smart phones for instant communication; electronic entertainment that replaces the company of other human beings; machines to do many of our daily chores; fast food for convenience (at the cost of our health). Let's be honest: if we get frustrated by a slow computer, we just go out and buy a faster one. We get frustrated if we have to wait in line at the store for just a little longer than usual. The truth is, our unhealthy lifestyles and even many of our world crises are signs of our impatience. Patience is a virtue, and we can correct those unhealthy habits by getting reconnected with the true, more patient nature that's in our hearts.

Learn from Nature

Nature can teach us the truth about harmonious living, as Lao Tzu emphasizes in the *Tao Te Ching*. He saw what nature offers mankind: the essence of yin and yang, reflecting the cosmic laws of the universe. If we only pay attention, we too will hear nature talk to us. Lao Tzu explained the art of leadership by observing the rivers and sea; we can apply his lessons to our own daily lives. An example of his writing is as follows, translated by Chao-Hsiu Chen:

> *Rivers and seas can be king of the hundred valleys, only because they accept their lower position. Therefore, they can be king of the hundred valleys.*
> *That is why the sage who wishes to rule the people must stay beneath them, who wishes to lead the people must follow behind them.*

In this way, the sage stays above the people, yet does not oppress them. He stays ahead of the people, yet does not exhaust them.

Then the people will support him with joy and never tire of following him.

And because he does not fight, no one can fight against him.

Chapter 5

Changing Destiny, Redefining Fate

Each man is the architect of his own fate.
—Appius Claudius

Is it possible to change your fate? Absolutely! Otherwise, it would defeat the purpose of the I Ching and feng shui, which were created to help us avoid danger and attract good luck. As Zen master Liao-Fan Yuan points out, it is possible to change your destiny when you fully understand the fundamental principles of its creation. When you do, you can make *your* life anything you want it to be. Yuan echoes the Buddhist texts' statement that average people are under the control of fate—their lives are predetermined to the end. However, we also can influence fate by the way we live our lives; hence fate will loosen its rigid rules for those who have awakened, especially when they have done a great many good deeds. Once these people have broken out of that bound state, they're positioned to be co-creators in their own destiny, redefining their own fates. So if you're wondering what your fate will be, take a closer look at all the things you do, because your fate truly is destined by karma.

Here's an analogy that helps describe how karma works under the law of cause and effect: think of it as a debt-and-reward point system. Bad deeds create debts, while good deeds generate rewards. However, demerit debts must be paid when they come due. Opportunities to win or lose points can show up under various circumstances in our lives; the bad and the good deeds can cancel each other out, or you can continue to accumulate more points on either side. The point value given to a certain deed, good or bad, depends on several factors, but the main one is the intention behind our action. The classic story of Robin Hood is a fine example of a genuine humanitarian whose conduct is criminal in the eyes of the law but is morally right because he's helping the weak. Therefore the merits he obtained from his deeds would surpass his deficits.

What this means is that we all have a chance to change our destiny in this lifetime simply by changing our state of mind. All you need is a positive intention and an effort to succeed. Believe it or not, we are often held back from our goals by our own habits and beliefs. Here are some common reasons why people fall short of achieving their dreams:

- They lack a goal or a clear vision.
- They're afraid of the unknown, or they have a fear of commitment.
- They're holding onto old habits and beliefs that don't work in their favor.
- They're focusing on things they don't want.
- They don't know how to change their thoughts.

And here's a simple formula for achieving your goals and dreams:
New Mind-Set = Changed Luck

Nuisance habits such as nail biting or compulsive blinking, self-sabotaging behaviors like gambling or compulsive shopping, and even more health-threatening habits like smoking or overeating can be overcome with self-help programs because these habits are largely mental, as opposed to more severe physical addictions that require medical attention. (In the latter instance, one should seek the advice of a physician.) Now, what we're discussing here is intended only as a suggestion for a self-help solution; it's not intended as medical advice. It's always best to consult a physician or counselor before you undertake a self-help regimen that you think might have an effect on your overall health.

So how do you get rid of your habits? Depriving your cravings by force is like taking a bottle from a hungry baby and not expecting a fight—it'll never work. The wise thing to do is to catch the habit at the beginning and correct it before it gets worse. Start by recognizing that everything we try for the first time has the potential to develop into a habit. When you're mindfully aware of this fact, you can stop a habit at an early stage.

But to improve your life permanently, you must get rid of the root cause of negative behavior, which is usually stress. You must abandon your old thought patterns and beliefs. Adopt new ways of thinking and acting; let go of everything that's been holding you down, including unhealthy attachments. I can assure you that you will feel better even if you only implement half the changes you should. You see, when we change our mind-set with proper intention, we allow our positive thoughts to expand. We open up our hearts and minds to new possibilities in our lives. Where there's faith, there's a miracle—when we think and believe intuitively, that is, we begin to see new ideas and promising solutions that we couldn't see before, even though they were there all the time. Before long, the law of cause and effect kicks in: each step we take leads to other positive feelings and opportunities, moving us closer to our goals and dreams than ever before.

Overcome Habits with the Power of Hypnotic Healing

Habits form character, and character is destiny.
—**Joseph Kaines**

Behaviorists have told us to look no further than our thought patterns to understand many of our unhealthy habits and life failures. For example, whenever we succumb to an uncontrollable urge of any kind, it is usually due to a lack of self-awareness, the result of repeated negative thoughts. Under certain conditions, those accumulated images and thoughts will develop into habits that in turn lead to addictions, which are very difficult to overcome.

Some behaviorists believe that these negative thought patterns may be hard-wired into our subconscious, usually without our realizing it. In that case, the subconscious is merely acting on what it knows. You might say these negative thoughts and actions are a function of our biology, especially through the secretion hormones. That explains why a person who has been abused in a prior relationship will tend to enter another abusive relationship. That's no surprise: we humans like to seek out other humans who emit familiar hormones like oxytocin (the hormone of love and comfort); researchers say some of us may even gravitate toward certain body odors. It's also not uncommon for people to surround themselves with what they hate most.

Sure, a sage will say it's heaven's will to put us in situations from which we need to learn—we need to figure things out on our own! It's no wonder so many of us fail to stick to our New Year's resolutions. Whether it's losing weight, quitting smoking, or getting better grades in school, it seems that we break the same promises year after year. We revert back to our old selves as our motivation wears off, and our willpower usually ditches us and costs us the victory. If we had to rely on willpower alone, our success in reaching our objectives would be very slim.

I know it's no easy task to change your habits—I've been there. But what if I told you there's a way to end them naturally, with no pain, with little or no struggle … would you be interested? I am sure you'll be delighted to hear that there's hope in your seemingly hopeless situation. We will explore a powerful method to help you that promises stunning results. It's the same process we've used to make our lives miserable—only now we are in control; redirecting energy for our benefit. We'll seize the power of our enemy, the ego self, and put our true self in charge. It's an incredibly effective technique; I've been using it to fix problem areas in my life, and it works like magic. So are you ready to change your own fate? Let's begin.

Allow me first to talk briefly about how we unwittingly develop these bad habits in the first place, so we have a better understanding of their mental underpinnings. Then we can recognize their existence and prevent such negative patterns from taking root in the future.

We know from medical research that people unconsciously develop strange behaviors when they're nervous or under stress. That dynamic gives rise to our bad habits. The behavioral symptoms are usually rooted in emotions like frustration, anger, resentment, anxiety, guilt, or shame. Cognitive behavioral therapy, and hypnotherapy have been used alongside conventional medicine to facilitate a speedy recovery from negative behavior patterns and to improve patients' quality of life.

Stress is also the leading contributing factor to depression-forming habits. It's a major culprit behind suicide and ill health. Stress has been linked to ulcers, kidney stones, cancer, and certain mental disorders. In general, it reduces the proper enjoyment of life. What happens biologically is a malfunction in both the nervous system and the endocrine system: stress causes an imbalance in our brain chemistry and weakens our immunity, leaving the body vulnerable to any attack. We all have different levels of stress tolerance. It is believed that about 10 percent of the world's population suffers from low stress tolerance. That means our negative energies are bumping into each other more often than we think.

Miscommunication among brain cells, again due to stress, leads to high levels of adrenaline, the "fight or flight" hormone. Adrenaline then overwhelms other chemicals essential to proper brain functioning, like the "feel-good" hormone dopamine. The result is depression. Stress has been identified as the main cause of sleep loss, due to its disruption of the body's production of serotonin, and it contributes to fatigue by disrupting production of noradrenalin in the brain. Stress is also one of the top sex-drive killers, as it can decrease libido by reducing oxytocin hormones; the result can be a strained relationship with your partner. A prolonged imbalance in brain chemistry will lead to more stress, which may in turn lead you to the edge of a complete nervous breakdown. Here are some symptoms to watch for:

- increased cravings
- feelings of guilt, resentment, fear, or anxiety
- panic attacks
- depression or withdrawal
- mood swings
- lack of restful sleep
- loss of energy or chronic exhaustion
- lack of interest in or enjoyment of daily activities
- aches and pains
- substance abuse
- destruct behavior toward self or family

There are many internal and external factors that can produce stress. Here are some common stressors that demand our close attention:

- financial issues
- unfulfilled desires and goals
- problems at work
- relationship problems
- negative habits or memories
- illness or aging
- restless sleep
- chronic weather concerns
- difficult commute
- environmental pollution: noise, odors, graphic images

An overactive brain is at risk of mental breakdown, which can result in serious injury or even death. It's imperative that we learn to cope with stress in today's fast-paced society. What's important is to find ways to control our stress that fit our individual situation; maintaining a healthy balance in the mind and body is crucial to our well-being and success. There are many among us who don't even know how to relax—because of our hectic work and lifestyles, we don't relax regularly enough to experience its benefits. Let's face it: two weeks of vacation a year isn't going to cut it. We must change our mind-set so that relaxation becomes a regular part of life and we don't need a vacation in order to enjoy it. Activities like sports, gardening, cleaning, dancing, or jogging are great ways to release stress buildup. Regular exercise and a balanced diet containing fruits and vegetables are important for keeping our stress level at bay. Researchers even suggest that safe, healthy sexual intimacy with your spouse or partner once or twice a week will increase your oxytocin levels. That can be a great stress buster, plus it will keep your romantic relationship alive and vigorous. Another health benefit of sex is that it increases your body's release of endorphins, a natural painkiller that will help relieve you of any physical aches and pains.

Other alternatives include meditation, chi-kung (qigong), tai chi, and yoga—great relaxation techniques you can practice every day to manage your stress and maintain inner peace. Of course, the best way to prevent a stressful life is not to create stress in the first place. That means giving up as many worldly attachments as possible, reducing the number of things you "must have." Foster your appreciation of life's basic pleasures. And don't let your pride control you: shed the three poisons within. Emotions are energies; any emotional illnesses can be overcome with positive emotions. I'll explain more about this in chapter 6, which describes the five elements cycles and principle.

We are now visiting the world of our subconscious mind—a place we rarely notice and almost never access deliberately. In order to enter this magical world, we must put ourselves into a deep, relaxing, altered state of consciousness such as an induced hypnosis or a trance. We'll do that naturally, of course, not with intoxicating substances. Once we've reached that state, we can implant the scripts (sets of instructions) of our intention by making positive suggestions and affirmations. Depending on the individual, sometimes all it takes is a few sessions and the subconscious will do as it's been programmed to do. Hypnosis is an ancient healing remedy—at least a few thousand years old. But it's very powerful stuff!

Teresa Moorey's *Working with Hypnotherapy* is a wonderful book if you want to practice self-hypnosis at home for self-healing. And Steve Ira Present, a neuro-linguistic specialist, has created many self-improvement programs that are very effective for helping you get rid of bad habits or make other positive life changes.

What is a trance? It is the first of three key factors required to develop a habit, good or bad. It is also the only gateway to our unconscious mind. Praying, meditation, and hypnosis are all techniques you can use to induce a hypnotic trance. You reach a calm, relaxed, hypnotic state of mind when you are completely mentally absorbed in something. That's when you're more open or susceptible to suggestions. It's possible to experience a trance even in our waking state—we've seen the effect from TV shows, especially kids' programs. We also see it in marketing and sales, with the hypnotic effects of infomercials, sales letters, books, and other forms of advertising. Induced trance is used alongside conventional medicine for pain management, and its effects are powerful. How powerful, you ask? I witnessed my own wife endure natural childbirth twice; her pain was eased with the help of trance.

By the way, this trancelike state is also the place where you can find and uproot any fears or phobias that may have been haunting you. What a great way to explore your inner self and heal at the same time!

Repetition is the second key factor in developing a habit. It's a way of programming a specific set of instructions in the brain for what you want it to do automatically. We form our core beliefs the same way. By repeating the same actions or thoughts over and over, they become hard-wired into our subconscious so they become second nature. It's like learning how to swim or ride a bicycle: once we learned, we don't have to think about it. (Perhaps you've noticed that I've been repeating some of the same information throughout this book. Well, now you know my motive!)

Emotional linking is the third factor in developing a habit. We are more likely to remember events that had a great impact on our lives than ones that didn't. So if we associate strong emotions with whatever it is that we're trying to accomplish, we'll get better results, because we've intentionally set up the right conditions for our new goal to match our positive experiences. Our objective here is to inspire self-confidence. We're instructing our subconscious to relive those good feelings from the past by bringing about new events that evoke those feelings.

Let's say you're looking for a job. It would be ideal, then, to evoke the good feelings you had when you landed your first job or were given a noteworthy promotion. Follow up with affirmation like this: *Employers are out there looking for skilled individuals like me, who will fit well into their workforce.* Carefully think out your affirmation, making sure to express it positively rather than skeptically. For example, instead of saying to yourself, *I don't want to look weak for my interview,* say, *I'm dressed for success today!*

Meditation: A True Path to Success and Long-Lasting Happiness

Sit quietly. Watch your thoughts and feelings pass in front of you. Relinquish control and the desire to get caught in them. See that nothing in life is permanent. Your thoughts, feelings, and perceptions all pass before you. If anything catches you, gently release it, and simply continue watching.
—**Zen Buddhist saying**

Besides all the health benefits we could gain from meditation, it is also vital to our chi (life force) and puts us in direct contact with our intuition, our higher true self (buddha-nature). Indeed, meditation is a significant mechanism for unlocking all sorts of negative energies that clutter our mind and body. The Tao says, "When the night is still, you can hear the silence. When the mind is still, listen to the silence and let it guide you." Wisdom is obtained not only from learning and contemplating (honest communication with oneself), but also from meditating. All great thinkers operate at this level of stillness. Their "Eureka moments" came from this state of mind. Ever notice that your most brilliant ideas come when you're most at peace? Think about it.

Meditation is one of the best ways to practice stillness. It puts you in a mental state of emptiness, unbounded by time or space, as described in Buddhist texts. During a meditative state, when you have successfully been made aware of your mind, you will exist only in the present moment, without the distraction of past or future. That should be the goal in your meditation practice.

Self-observation brings clarity, which leads to self-realization; through this you will overcome self-delusions. As you sit quietly in your meditative setting, ask for guidance. Spend some time in self-reflection, which will help you understand the true meaning of life. According to Zen wisdom,

"Whatever happens to you does not matter; what you've become through experiences is most important."

There are various forms of meditation, all with the same objective: to make you calm, relaxed, focused, composed, and free of negative emotions. Simple breathing techniques work best for some people, but others may feel comfortable with the visualization method or guided meditation, and some people also incorporate yoga or tai chi in their practice. Consider using a combination of different techniques, which can do wonders. Whatever method you choose, meditation is very beneficial, especially in today's fast-moving and economically stressful world. Meditation can help us slow down so we don't suffer from information overload. It makes tranquil the hostile mind, tames the ungratified heart, and balances the body. It also reduces stress, allowing the brain much-needed downtime and bringing us back to the center, where we have critical chi balance.

Meditate on the idea of selflessness—there's no *I* in *you*. The sky and the ocean are extensions of you, just as you are one with the universe. There are no boundaries between you and everything around you. Meditate on the idea of impermanence: what goes up must come down; what comes before you will soon pass; and what now exists will cease in time. So, too, will your habits, as will your illusory emotions of fear, hate, anger, or guilt. They are all under your control and will be dissolved once you let them go. Meditation will put you in a position to release any negative energy that exists inside you. It will help you develop a stronger, more vibrant aura (body energy field) that is vital to your health and well-being.

Meditate to the energy of a mandala, one of many sacred symbols of God; it is associated with wholeness in many religions, and it is known to have profound healing effects on the seeker who is pursuing good health and happiness. This mystical symbol of the creation of the universe appears in many different forms. For example, we see it in nature, in the sun, moon, stars, and galaxies. It appears in landforms and in architectural forms and landscapes on religious grounds. *Mandala* means "sacred circle" in Sanskrit, and we know it has long had special meaning to humans, as we have learned from the history of geoglyphs. More mandalas—giant, wheel-shaped stone structures—were recently discovered in the Middle East. The symbolic meaning of the circle, used throughout human history, is fascinating and mysterious. For example, we have the circle of life, the circle of time, and even circular rituals and dance ceremonies. We use the metaphor of the circle in our places of worship and our communities (such as "social circles"). A mandala is often used as a feng shui tool for healing in the home or workplace.

Visualize yourself as the light of love and compassion radiating in all directions, diffused within you and the world around you. This higher energy level is very effective for healing your own pain or benefiting those experiencing difficulty in their lives. Here are some known benefits of regular meditation:

- It helps you develop intuitive insight and wisdom.
- You gain direct access to the powerful subconscious mind.
- It helps you calm down, relax, and attain tranquility or inner peace.
- It heightens your awareness of your environmental energy.
- It encourages clear vision and concentration, creativity, and problem solving.
- It releases negative emotions, distress, and resistance trapped within you.
- It defuses the three poisons: greed, hatred, and ignorance.
- It invokes healing powers, relieving stress and depression.
- It promotes balanced brain chemistry and boosts immunity.
- It facilitates restful sleep.
- It promotes the health of mind, body, and spirit, including biological function and circulation.
- It keeps you grounded and centered, connected with your spirituality.

Meditation comes in many forms and various levels of difficulty. Test each technique and adjust it to your liking. Dawn is the best time to meditate, but you may choose to do it whenever you're most comfortable, as long as you're consistent. Proper breathing is important to meditation; counting your breath is the simplest and most common way to start your practice. Since we are an air-breathing species, the air we breathe helps sustain life—we need oxygen to turn chemical energy (food) into usable energy for body function. Breathing exercises remind us that this gift from nature is precious, and that we should take good care of it, just as it has taken care of us.

Plan to work two five-minute meditation sessions into your daily schedule—preferably one at midday. Then gradually lengthen each session as your concentration skills improve. Commit to a thirty-minute session each day, aiming for an ultimate goal of an hour or longer. Adjust your mind-set so you're prepared to enjoy each session wholeheartedly, as opposed to forcing yourself into it. If you love what you're doing, each obstacle will become just another opportunity for trying new experiments. You'll find that learning new things is a lifelong adventure.

Plan your entire session so you're completely free of distractions. Begin in a comfortable sitting posture, eyes closed or slightly opened. Take a few deep breaths and then relax. Focus on your breath, concentrating on the rise and fall of your diaphragm as you breathe in and out. Begin counting with each inhalation, ending with ten as you finish exhaling. Repeat the whole process with each breath. Whenever you're distracted by thoughts, memories, images, noises, conversation, or emotions, simply acknowledge them and return to your breathing. With practice, you will experience stillness and serenity, and in no time you will have successfully obtained inner peace.

Abdominal breathing (or "deep breathing") is crucial in chi-kung exercise. Not only is it the correct way to breathe, but it strengthens our immunity by replenishing our lungs with quality air containing the vital cosmic chi. It enhances life-force energy by removing trapped, stagnant air in the lungs and encouraging chi flow around the body for our well-being. Chinese medicine suggests that stronger lungs will lead to a more vital respiratory system, which in turn benefits our thinking, emotions, sexual energy, skin, and senses. As we become calmer as a result of better circulation and clearer thoughts, we find that we don't get angry as often. That's because we're less depressed and have more courage with which to face our problems. Furthermore, the natural cycle theory of Chinese medicine links healthy lungs to healthier kidneys, which most certainly will have a good impact on our physical and mental performance.

Here's how you do abdominal breathing, as taught by Master Wong Kiew Kit:

Stand upright with both feet fairly close together; drop both hands straight down to your sides. Clear your thoughts and relax your body, as in a meditative state. Start by breathing in deeply and gently with your nose all the way down into the lower abdomen, filling it up as you would inflate a balloon. Hold the breath for two or three seconds, and then exhale slowly and completely through your mouth to empty out all air from your abdomen. As you breathe in and out, imagine that the air is supreme universal energy, cleansing and removing toxins as it replaces all stagnant chi. It then passes from your lungs into your lower abdomen, cleansing and recycling all the negative emotions there. Then out goes the bad chi through your mouth as you exhale completely. Repeat this process for five to ten minutes once or twice every day.

There are many forms of chi-kung exercises to bring together in harmony your body's "three treasures"—*jing* (essence), *chi* (energy), and *shen* (spirit). In doing so, they generate a vibrant, healthy body and mind. According to Taoist philosophy, advanced practices can lead to a strong, protective chi that works like body armor, as seen with Shaolin kung fu. Through further development of these skills, you can obtain psychic powers, performing what we call miracles—achieving out-of-body experiences or transmitting *chi* to someone a thousand miles away, as demonstrated by skilled chi-kung masters in the past few decades. At the highest level of Tao you achieve sainthood. Obviously, imagination or visualization is critical and powerful tool, a gift that all humans have. Chi-kung incorporates it extensively into all its exercise and meditation techniques.

Visualization meditation is a technique that uses your imagination or creative faculty to achieve results. For example, if you pick a colorful mandala as your meditative object, you would begin by examining it in great detail, starting with the outer circle and gradually moving toward the center. Concentrate on its colors, sizes, shapes, patterns, etc., and then close your eyes and recreate the entire image in your mind. Meditating on a mandala can help us find the answers we seek, and it can dissolve old memories or feelings from early childhood, especially those filled with fears and guilt that somehow impacted our character development.

There are various forms of gazing meditation. Candle gazing is unique method: without blinking, you look intensely into the focal point of a candle's flame until you weep like a baby. Tears will pour from your eyes. Gazing intensely into the reflected light of quartz crystal is another fascinating way to achieve deep meditation. You experience a deep sense of the present moment while feeling spiritually connected at the same time.

To reap the full rewards of meditation, gradually incorporate various techniques into your own practice. Perhaps with the help of quartz crystals you can heighten your spiritual awareness as you experiment to see what works best for you. Whatever combination of techniques you choose, make sure to blend meditation and self-hypnosis for a most rewarding experience, because one works directly with your spirituality in the present moment, the here and now, while the other removes the negativity of the past so you can begin constructively changing your future. You'll also find that breaking bad habits is easier than ever—that's a promise! Having said all that, I'd like to leave you with a quote from Confucius: "The more man meditates upon good thoughts, the better will be his world and the world at large." Let's all meditate on that thought.

Creative Visualization and Affirmation

Are there any effective techniques for helping us change our mind-set? Psychological research suggests that the power of our imagination is much greater than our willpower, which is why healers so often incorporate creative visualization into their practices. Its sole purpose is to help us achieve success and reach ours goals; it's like a mind-programming tool. Creative visualization mainly involves meditative exercises in which you use nothing but your imagination to construct chains of mental events like scenes in a movie, complete with themes, settings, and a happy ending reflecting the desired results. This technique is used as a complement to conventional medicine for healing chronic diseases. What it does, essentially, is change the body chemistry using the awesome healing power of the mind. You might say it's the same as chi-kung when applied as a healing approach—it focuses directly upon the root cause of the problem. It's just that simple!

Affirmation is often used in feng shui as a kind of trigger to invoke higher energy and attract it into our homes and our lives. Affirmation can come in any symbolic form, like images, writing, characters, numbers, figures, or chants. Similar to hypnosis, meditative affirmation is a process of repeating positive words or phrases enough to encode or program them onto our subconscious, replacing negative thoughts, behaviors, or habits. Through affirmation, we can carefully and consciously craft powerful words or scripts that we repeat in order to make us feel good and raise our energy or dopamine level.

Say I wanted to share my work experience with others. Instead of saying, "Many people will be interested in my work," I would say, "Millions of people all over the world are captivated by my work because it's helping them see new possibilities in their lives and transform hardships into miraculous, happy events." I've done two things with that new statement: first, I've given myself a target by mentioning a more specific number, and second,

I've changed the sentence to present tense to appease the subconscious, which does not operate in the past or the future. My subconscious now has clear, precise instructions for how to effect a transformation. All I need to do now is put my total trust in the cosmic law of cause and effect; I know something magical is coming together in my life because I have already created a cause (the work), so its effects (people) will surely follow. I've also prepared myself to accept and feel content with the result, however dramatic.

Avoid using words like *don't* or *no* and phrases like *I don't want*, because chances are you will get what you don't want, and we don't want that, do we? (I know—it's a weak joke.) Ever notice how teachers and lifeguards yell "Walk!" to kids in the hallway or by the pool? That's because "Don't run!" seems to be counter-effective. Simply put, you get what you focus on. So choose inspiring words and phrases that you know are true and consistent with whatever it is you're attempting to change. For example, instead of saying to yourself, *I don't want to fight with my partner anymore*, think, *I know we can find a happy medium to resolve the situation.* Notice that the first statement reflects frustration that translates into stress as well as negative energy that fuels the ego. Meanwhile, your subconscious focuses on the key word *don't*, which is filled with emotion. This creates friction and resistance within yourself, and of course fighting with your ego never gets you anywhere.

Here's what happened with my revised statement: I created higher-energy vibrations with images and thoughts I can agree with and accept as my new beliefs. Essentially, I've broken that continuous cycle of negativity—removing conflicting signals and blockages residing or building up inside me.

Yoga meditation does the same thing: it makes us aware of harmful energies in our body and mind, removing them to prevent a complete shutdown. Yoga exercises appease all three systems critical to our well-being: body, mind, and spirit. Besides yoga, there are two other wonderful methods of meditation for those who have problems maintaining a still posture: tai chi chuan and chi-kung. Both involve close observation of the perpetual flow of life-force energy, which nature brings into harmony and balance to sustain life on earth. Tai chi forms originated from chi-kung and are considered moving meditation; they promote the continuous flow of yin-yang or internal-external energy throughout the body. Energy flows along the meridians to maintain a balanced chi—removing blocked energy and connecting mind, body, and spirit (intuitive wisdom). Chi-kung does not always involve continuous movement, but its concepts are very much in tune with tai chi techniques. Chi-kung has been known to cure severe diseases and has been used as an anesthetic in surgery. All three methods of meditation—yoga, tai chi, and chi-kung—encourage the free flow of chi throughout the body's chakra channels to promote well-being (see diagram 5.1).

To see immediate results from your efforts, it's most effective to include meditation, self-hypnosis, and affirmation in your practice every day. Believe me, you will be amazed at what you can do.

True knowledge or intuitive wisdom can be attained just through the daily practice of meditation. A wise man once told his student that no matter how many good deeds he did, he would never break out of the cycle of rebirth, suffering, and death until he succeeded in meditation. The Buddha himself would never have been able to obtain enlightenment had he not abandoned his old ways and adopted meditation. Meditation is a nonreligious technique, so everyone should feel comfortable practicing it.

The simplest meditation pose is the seated one you see from the popular Buddha statues. Do this once or twice a day for fifteen minutes each session. Sit up straight or with a back support, legs crossed. Rest your left hand on top of your right, both palms facing up, thumbs touching on the tips to create a "sacred bowl" shape, a symbol of the Buddhist philosophy of non-attachment promoting peace, happiness, and prosperity. Close your eyes or keep them slightly open, looking down, and focus on a single point. Meditate using the simple breathing technique or one of the other techniques we've already discussed. At the very least, you will feel the simple joy of just *being*—doing nothing at the present but enjoying a quiet, peaceful, relaxing moment with nothing else on your mind. Ahhh …

Tap into the Healing Energy of Nature

Nature is our best healer—naturally. Its healing properties are powerful, and they can be harnessed for our benefit. We all know the soothing sound of a gentle stream, the refreshing fragrance of fresh flowers, the enchanting or even breathtaking sight of ocean-side cliffs or towering mountains. An array of colorful plants, shrubs, and trees can mesmerize our senses, and the mystic moon holds powers that somehow affect our behavior. It should be no surprise to anyone that bringing nature into our home in the proper place creates good feng shui.

Trees and plants are natural healers. Wood energy is growth—it's like the liver, the only organ that can regrow itself. So whenever you feel bogged down by bad luck, you can find relief under a tree. Spending some time under a pine or an oak can help release any inner negative energy while replenishing your life force. In her book *Moon Spells*, Diane Ahlquist presents a list of trees and their curative powers, (e.g., the walnut tree heals infertility and depression, the pecan tree helps with job searches and money opportunities, and the plum tree enhances love and relationships).

Since the beginning of humanity, natural precious stones have been used for tools, shelters, communication, and jewelry—and they've even made their way into today's technological world of computers and gadgetry. But did you know that stones are still being used today for healing purposes? Jennie Harding covered this subject in one of her books, *Crystals*, a worthwhile exploration of some of nature's most beautiful objects and their amazing healing powers. Jasper, for example, has been used for grounding and protecting the body while strengthening the aura. Tigereye, a semiprecious stone, is used for energizing the body, enhancing sexual energy, clearing mental blockages, and strengthening the eyesight. Wearing emerald or jade jewelry is said to have healing effects on the whole body and mind, not to mention awesome protective powers. Green is a symbol of growth, vitality, and renewal; it is associated with the heart in the chakra system. It is used to balance the energies in the kidneys and circulatory system, support liver function, encourage tissue repair, and promote peace and love in the home.

It's believed that holding or wearing quartz crystals, or placing them on the body along the chakras while meditating, will do wonders for the whole body. Crystals are said to contain healing properties that are especially pertinent to emotional illnesses. They are good, natural elements that can harmonize with surrounding energies, even attracting good luck. Amethysts are beautiful crystals that are used to calm the nervous system, ease stress and headaches, and improve sleep. They heighten our spiritual awareness and open the wisdom eye ("third eye"). Rose crystals bring harmony to the heart, attracting and encouraging romantic relationships and compassion in our lives, and easing emotional stress like fear or nervous tension. According to Ahlquist, moonstones have dazzling powers to balance feminine energy when worn over the heart, and they harmonize mind and body during periods of hormonal change like menstruation, puberty, and menopause. They also are a remedy for infertility.

Make an effort to exploit these natural beauties in meditation or during relaxation sessions. Use them as feng shui cures in the home or workplace, or wear them as jewelry. The above-mentioned crystals are affordable in small sizes and are readily available at your local feng shui or jewelry store. While visiting the Grand Canyon, I found really good-sized stones at Valle Travel Stop in Williams, Arizona. You may also want to browse online at BestCrystals.com and GemSelect.com.

Sea salt contains minerals that can dispel negative environmental influences. Spread or place it in areas of the home or business where negative energy may be gathering—it makes a good feng shui cure for cleansing bad vibes from the air. (You can locate negative areas by paying attention to where your cat likes to sit and rest—cats tend to attract to offensive energy.)

When used properly, scents can dramatically awaken our senses and quite often even alter our mood. Pleasant scents offer a great way to disperse stagnant negative energy while elevating pure cosmic energy in and around the home. Try using essential oils, which are produced for a variety of applications—just make sure to check with the manufacturer for any side effects or allergic reactions if you plan to use them in your home or workplace.

There are many health benefits from the use of natural essential oils in aromatherapy. Pine oil, for example, has been used to ease mental stress and elevate mood, relieving anxiety and nervous tension. It also has been used to increase metabolism, fight infection, and soothe respiratory problems like cold, flu, allergies, and sinus congestion, and dermatologists sometimes use it as a rejuvenating skin treatment. Rosemary and eucalyptus oils are natural remedies used to treat stress disorders, nervous tension, memory loss, cough, asthma, bronchitis, and sinus problems. The scent of lavender has a calming effect on the nervous system; it's a great remedy for insomnia and body pains and aches. Cedar wood and tea tree oil are just two of the many essential oils with highly medicinal properties. These oils are used for a wide variety of purposes: as antiseptic, antiviral, or anti-spasmodic treatments; as insecticides; for toxin removal; for treatment of pain, high blood pressure, or menstrual irregularities; and to boost the immune system, among other purposes. Grapefruit is known as a great antioxidant; it stimulates the endocrine and nervous systems and removes toxic waste from the body while benefiting the organ systems, skin, and hair. Lemon and orange oils have similar properties; lemon, especially, boosts brain function, while orange oil has a natural sedative agent to combat depression while helping you relax. To find out more about the benefits of essential oils, visit OrganicFacts.net.

The colors of the spectrum have been used very effectively in healing therapy for thousands of years. Each color's healing properties are said to have their own wavelength and frequency vibrations, with each color in the visible spectrum corresponding to one of the seven colors of the rainbow in the chakra system: red, orange, yellow, green, blue, indigo, and violet. This is only a tiny part of the whole electromagnetic spectrum, yet it has played an important role in civilizations throughout human history. It has been incorporated into a wide range of Taoist teachings, from the I Ching, divination, astrology, and feng shui to the Chinese medicine wheel and martial arts. In feng shui, color is part of the five elements theory. In holistic healing, the colors of the spectrum can be used as stimulants in areas linked to the chakras. Visit ColourTherapyHealing.com to explore the wonders of color therapy.

It is generally accepted that energy from the moon can impact our mood and alter our behavior. Why not learn from the expert in this subject? Diane Ahlquist shows us how to harvest the moon's mysterious powers for our benefit, planning and undertaking important tasks that can correspond with the powers of each moon phase. For example, a dark moon is a perfect time for ourselves. A crescent moon encourages new beginnings and new ventures, like job interviews. A waxing moon is good for planning a romantic evening or asking someone out on a date, while a waning moon is a time to letting go, like old habits and old beliefs, and a full moon creates ideal conditions for working on new commitments in your life. Even if you're not a believer in that kind of mysterious lunar magic, look to the Chinese lunar calendar when planning your next special events. A full version of the calendar offers details incorporating feng shui and astrology, the five elements principle, and do's and don'ts for the year, months, days, and hours. Of course, use the information sparingly so that it does not severely hamper the way you live your life.

The Chakra System

Chakras are the source of an intangible life force or "energy of consciousness"; they are invisible, like the meridians (pathways of energy flow). In their book *Healing with Crystals and Chakra Energies*, Sue and Simon Lilly describe how chakras work in the endocrine system, glands, nerves, blood vessels, lymph nodes, etc., at the physical level. The chakra system is our individual spiritual life energy focused through channels that begin at the base of the spine and end at the crown of the head. There are seven concentrated energy centers (called "wheels" in Sanskrit) that run along the front of the body or the spinal column as described in the practice of yoga. These chakra points are vital energy fields; they also appear on the "conception vessel" meridians identified in Taoist chi-kung philosophy.

Sue and Simon Lilly explain how the chakra system represents seven stages of growth and development, starting at conception and ending when we reach adulthood. This cycle repeats itself throughout our lifetime.

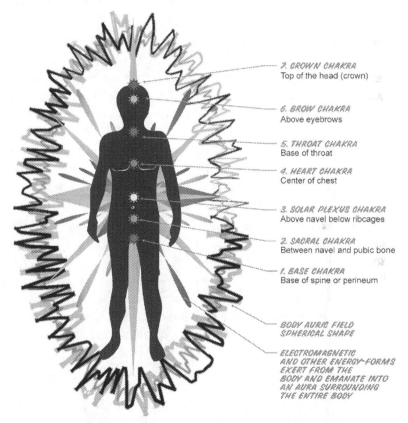

7. CROWN CHAKRA
Top of the head (crown)

6. BROW CHAKRA
Above eyebrows

5. THROAT CHAKRA
Base of throat

4. HEART CHAKRA
Center of chest

3. SOLAR PLEXUS CHAKRA
Above navel below ribcages

2. SACRAL CHAKRA
Between navel and pubic bone

1. BASE CHAKRA
Base of spine or perineum

BODY AURIC FIELD
SPHERICAL SHAPE

ELECTROMAGNETIC
AND OTHER ENERGY-FORMS
EXERT FROM THE
BODY AND EMANATE INTO
AN AURA SURROUNDING
THE ENTIRE BODY

HUMAN AURA AND THE CHAKRA SYSTEM

Diagram 5.1 *Seven areas of energy concentration or "consciousness" aligned along the front of the body or spinal column in a Hindu chakra system.*

According to Chinese medicine, our body organs are developed in the order of their existence. After birth they regulate both our bodily functions and our spirituality, and they guide us to the spiritual lessons we ought to learn as we grow older. It's only natural that we get imbalances in our chakra system from time to time; energies simply cannot flow freely when we're tense. If a serious buildup occurs, we will begin to show signs of chronic symptoms in parts of our body that correspond with the affected chakra points. Now, if we ever become seriously ill, there are things we can and must do ourselves while also getting the necessary medical attention. After all, complete healing requires not only the help of medical professionals but our own participation. The Lillys explain how each of the seven chakra points affects us physically, mentally, and spiritually.

The benefits of learning the chakra system are reinforced by Taoist wisdom. Chi-kung Master Zongxian Wu teaches simple exercises that can help us connect to the universal energy source. In one of his books, *Chinese Shamanic Cosmic Orbit Qigong*, he shows how these exercises directly link to the chakra system for self-cultivation and self-healing. The exercises focus on the mind, spirit, and body, working together with yin-yang energy and the five energies of the creation of the universe. Regularly practicing these exercises promotes the free circulation of life energy (chi) to enhance our physical vitality, control our emotions, and essentially eradicate the three poisons. His lessons involve seated meditation that incorporates a charm symbol, mantras (voice vibration), mudras (hand gestures), breathing, and visualization to achieve excellent results.

Each of the seven chakra points serves a distinct purpose:

Base chakra rules our instinct to survive, enabling us to function as human beings. It is the energy behind natural impulses necessary for the existence of any species, like reproduction and hoarding. Base chakra is associated with the adrenal glands and relates to our sense of awareness. When imbalanced, it can lead to insecurity and fearfulness that exhibits as stress—manifested either as withdrawal or aggression. Self-denial, anger, and low motivation are usually signs of insufficient energy in the base chakra. Traditional Chinese medicine (TCM) calls this point Huiyin, The Gate of Life and Death, or the perineum. Taoist chi-kung theory introduced by Master Wong Kiew Kit refers to this vital energy channel as the seat of *Jing* (essence). When properly maintained, this energy reservoir will lengthen one's life.

Sacral chakra regulates our emotions and how we express ourselves; emotional tension accumulates here. This is the most vital chi reservoir, as it connects to sexual energy and the reproductive system; it is associated with the sex glands. It is critical that we take care of the kidneys, as that's where our life energy source is stored. Strong kidneys will make us not only feel young, but also look young. TCM calls this area *Qihai*, "the sea of chi," and Taoist chi-kung also refers to this point as "the seat of chi" (the origin of life energy or life force). By focusing on the sacral chakra you can work to change your life as well as your karma, finding joy and serenity, as suggested by Master Wu.

Solar plexus chakra relates to personal power—it involves the personality and the ego. On the one hand it nurtures the self, giving us a sense of security and optimism. On the other it challenges our self-worth, bringing down our self-esteem. It is associated with the adrenal glands and the pancreas.

Heart chakra is also referred to as "the mind" by ancient Taoists. It's connected with love and the integration of spirit and body that generates the expression of love and compassion for ourselves and others. It gives you the power to give and receive love unconditionally. This is the fertile, empty space that gives birth to new creations. Work on this area to release any negative energy that may have been generated by the three poisons. The heart chakra is associated with the thymus gland; TCM refers to it as "the sea of tranquility." Connect with this point for balancing your emotions and calming your mind and spirit. Taoist chi-kung refers to this point as "spirit," the first point of the Seats of Shen. It is associated with the consciousness. Master Wu shows us "Embracing Infinity" chi-kung exercises to help us work on this particular point—here, "resonating with the Dao," we can work to purify our heart, develop true compassion, and accept things as they are.

Throat chakra is the center of our communication and creativity. We must learn to express the truth about our needs and desires because others will judge us based on our expressions. The throat chakra is directly linked to the thyroid glands.

Brow (wisdom-eye or third-eye) chakra directs our intuitions, thoughts, and imagination. Intuitive wisdom helps us see things as they are, guiding us to accept and let go of attachments. The brow chakra is associated with the pineal gland that produces and regulates melatonin for the proper functioning of the endocrine and nervous systems. It is the "body clock" that oversees sleep patterns and body temperature. It is widely known as the portal to the spirit world. The brow chakra, or the mind, is the second point to the Seats of Shen.

Crown chakra is also referred to as "the heart" by ancient Taoists. It is the consciousness (spirit), the control center of our senses. It allows us to connect with our spirituality and the universal life force, guiding us to live in the present and not be restrained by the past or future. It is associated with wisdom and knowledge, and it directs us on the right path. The crown chakra links to the pituitary gland, which produces the endocrine hormones, such as growth hormone, dopamine, estrogen, oxytocin, and endorphins. These hormones are essential to our proper growth, blood pressure, temperature, sex organs, and thyroid function, among other anatomical systems. Crown chakra is Taoist chi-kung's third, vital point in the Seats of Shen. It is associated with Baihui, which connects the third-eye and heart chakras.

The Meridian System

The ancient sages recognized that humans and the universe are manifestations of chi, the force responsible for creating and sustaining all life forms and everything else as well. This cosmic force is referred to variously, depending on the context—it's also been called Tao, energy, and life force. Chi is invisible and intangible; it is both external and internal. Outside the body, chi-kung masters refer to it as cosmic energy. Inside the body, chi is known to contain electromagnetic forces, infrared rays, electricity, light, heat, and charged particles that give it powerful energy. Taoist philosophers suggest that our body is a microcosm of the universe, with chi acting as the medium that connects us all. In other words, there are no boundaries between you, me, and the universe. Everything is interconnected, from one cell or organ in the body to another, from one meridian to the next. My thoughts affect your body chemistry as well as my own; they reach from my own circle of family and friends to yours and on to the whole world. According to Taoist principle, a higher being is capable of interacting with, controlling, or manipulating the chi of another person. This level of understanding is reached only by a small number of people, but it is possible, even for an ordinary person, to obtain such skills with varying degrees of success.

In the medical philosophy of Taoist chi-kung and its descendent, traditional Chinese medicine, there are twelve main meridians or pathways that connect to the organs, carrying vital chi throughout the body. Meanwhile, eight other meridians store energy that can be tapped when the body needs it. When a person is sick, it is thought that the energy flow is blocked in certain parts of the body meridians, resulting in an imbalance in the body system or organs. If the problem is neglected it will require medical attention. Since our internal organs can be directly accessed by our external body parts, as suggested by the five elements theory, it is likely that this unhealthy chi can be manifested in the person's physical appearance, such as the skin or face; pain provides another hint at what is happening to us internally. And remember that a frail body will generate a weak and distorted aura that can further diminish your protection from unhealthy external forces in the environment.

There are two main meridians you should get to know if you want vibrant health and a keen spirit. There's the yin channel, the conception meridian, which connects all the spiral energy centers at the front of our body, similar to the chakra system, and the yang channel, the governing meridian, which connects the spiral energy centers at the back to complete the system of energy flow. Daily chi-kung deep-breathing exercises combined with meditation will keep these and other internal organ meridians free-flowing and filled with vibrant life energy.

But chi-kung exercise is perhaps my favorite natural healing practice for vital health and curing illness. Chi-kung practitioners have made compelling claims about its usefulness for preventing diseases. Master Wong Kiew Kit, in his book *The Art of Chi Kung*, provides great insight into chi-kung philosophy and offers simple exercises. He also introduces advanced techniques that use mind over matter to perform physical tasks that would seem impossible to the untrained person. (You may have already seen them in the spectacular displays of Shaolin kung fu.)

For most of us, however, our goals should be aimed at training our mind and body for health purposes; understanding the wisdom of treating one emotion with another can have phenomenal effects on body function. For example, Master Wong demonstrates what I refer to as "internal feng shui," which applies to the underlying emotions. He reminds us that we can apply the principles of the five elements cycle as follows: A happy event (Fire) can overcome our misery (Metal). Meanwhile grief can defuse our anger (Wood), and as hatred subsides, our compassion (Fire) will emerge—just as tragic events generally bring people together. Diagram 6.1 gives us a visual understanding of the interplay among the five elements, which connect to emotions and the body organs.

The five organs are considered the center of emotional feelings, and they are governed by the five elements as follows:

- **Heart:** the seat of intellect
- **Liver:** the center of feelings, the sanctuary of the soul
- **Stomach:** the seat of learning, the storehouse of truth
- **Lungs:** the seat of righteousness
- **Kidneys:** the seat of survival, the storehouse for vital life energy

We should always be aware that our emotional state can have great impact on our organs and bodily functions. The table below shows how the five elements constantly affect our emotions and our health. Also, refer to the five elements tables in chapter 6 for other elemental associations that help combat negative emotions. For example, the eye reveals the health of the liver; the tongue reveals the health of the heart; the mouth reveals the health of the abdominal organs; the nose reveals the health of the lungs; and the ear reveals the health of the kidneys.

If you are experiencing difficulty in any of these areas, try combining different types of meditation. A simple but effective technique I use to remove blockages is to visualize my palms as charged with cosmic energy while placing them onto the chakra points or along the two main meridians. Placing natural stones onto the chakra points during a deep relaxation session can release underlying negative emotions and help speed up the healing process.

Table 5a Emotions and The Five Elements				
Anger (Wood)	Joy (Fire)	Worry (Earth)	Grief (Metal)	Fear (Water)
Affects:	Affects:	Affects:	Affects:	Affects:
Liver and Gall Bladder	Heart and Small Intestine	Stomach and Spleen	Lung and Large Intestine	Kidneys and Urine-Bladder
Caused by:	Caused by:	Caused by:	Caused by:	Caused by: Lack of knowledge,
Obsessive desires, greed, frustration, aggression, competitive	Extreme excitement. Problem with self-expression and communication	Uncertain, Lack of Self-confident, Nurturing or caring	Loss— Having trouble accepting and letting go	Fear of loss, rejection, or control Low energy level
How to improve:	How to improve:	How to improve:	How to improve:	How to improve:
Generosity, kindness, contentment	Patience, compassion	Calm, open, acceptance	Courage	Wisdom, gentleness
Remedies— Meditation/stimulant:	Remedies— Meditation/stimulant:	Remedies— Meditation/stimulant:	Remedies— Meditation/stimulant:	Remedies— Meditation/stimulant:
Chakras: Crown and Sacral Chakras.	Chakras: Crown, Brow, Heart, and Throat Chakras.	Chakras: Solar Plexus, Sacral, and Base Chakras.	Chakras: Crown, Brow, Throat, Heart, and Base Chakras.	Chakras: Sacral, Brow, and Base Chakras.
Color: Violet and Orange	Colors: Violet, indigo, and green, blue	Color: Red, orange, yellow	Color: Violet, indigo, blue, and green	Color: Indigo, orange and red
Stones: Clear quartz crystal, Amethyst, Moonstone, Citrine quartz	Stones: Clear quartz, Amethyst, Moonstone, Red Ruby, Rose quartz, Green Emerald and Jade	Stones: Clear quartz crystal, Moonstone, Citrine quartz	Stones: Clear quartz crystal, Amethyst quartz crystal, Emerald, Red Ruby, Smoky	Stones: Clear quartz, Amethyst, Citrine, Moonstone, Smoky, and agate
Aromas & Essential Oils: Lavender, Pine, Mandarin, Rosemary, Chamomile	Aromas & Essential Oils: Rosemary, Lavender, Pine, Majoram, Mandarin	Aromas & Essential Oils: Lavender, Bergamot, Pine, Franincense	Aromas & Essential Oils: Lavender, Bergamot, Rose, Pine, Ylang, Rosemary	Aromas & Essential Oils: Lavender, Mandarin, Chamomile, Pine

Here Master Wong (like many others) suggests that a healthy, fit person who is full of vitality and feels young even in old age has a good balance of the three treasures, shen, chi, and jing, which serve to unify the physical body and the spirit. Shen is the consciousness that controls our life-force energy (chi) and body cells (jing). The three are closely interrelated, so when one is weak it will affect the other two. When a person feels depressed, for example, he or she is said to have a cloudy shen, which will weaken chi, creating blockages in the circulation that affect the immune system and other body organs (jing) from functioning normally. The base chakra belongs to Seat of Jing; the sacral chakra belongs to Seat of Chi; and the heart, wisdom-eye, and crown chakras are grouped together as the Seats of Shen. They all must work in harmony with one another.

So there you have it, folks: we've just uncovered the true magic in the art of living. It's time to get acquainted with a variety of sensational tools for self-improvement. These ancient wisdoms are timeless, and they contain immense healing powers—quite ordinary but potent! The path to your happiness and your true destiny is laid out before you. The degree to which you succeed in making your dreams a reality falls upon you and no one else. Your vision, passion, and actions are equally important factors in your success. Listen with your heart, always being mindful of your emotions, conduct, and behavior. Wisdom gained through self-realization will ensure you are on the right path. Meditate on the heart and mind, and given time, your body chemistry will shift and your awareness will be heightened. Then you will be on the right path to reach enlightenment.

Listen to your body. Your physical and psychological pain, your body temperature, the appearance of your face and skin, and even your body odors are ways your body communicates with you. Take the necessary action to address those conditions. Reduce stress buildup, as that destroys life energy. Another implication of your symptoms may be that you are ready to reconnect with a part of your higher self, or to your god. Ancient wisdom teaches us not to fight the prevailing current but to accept what may have already become reality at this very moment in our life. Furthermore, we must have the courage to accept and adapt to new circumstances, learning from them and making the necessary changes, just as we live with the changing seasons but adapt accordingly. By doing so, we can prevent negative energy buildup from stress, removing our inner struggles rather than creating even more resistance.

You can be your own fortune-teller. Look to the present if you want to know your future: what you're doing right here and now is ultimately creating the framework for your future. If you don't like what you see in your destination, then change what you are doing right at this moment. In other words, make adjustments to your desires in order to change your destiny. Everything has its order, its proper time and place—and when you've done everything right in accordance with the law of cause and effect, it's only a matter of time before your rewards will come to you. The opposite also holds true: if whatever you're doing is unethical and wicked, brace yourself for the wrath of heaven. In the end, you'll have no one to blame but yourself.

Above all, when I feel greed starting to take control, I remind myself that real abundance comes from the simplest things in life. Now go right ahead with your dreams: cast a wonderful spell for yourself and set up some good inner feng shui to create optimum conditions for success. But when you open your eyes and mind with patience and trust, you will see magic gradually unfold in your life, day after day. Ahhh, isn't that a beautiful feeling?

Part II

Chapter 6

The Truth about Feng Shui

The Five Kinds of Luck That Impact Your Life

Now that you've taken care of your state of mind, you undoubtedly understand that the first critical step to creating good feng shui is placing it within yourself. These next few chapters will focus on how to place feng shui outside yourself—how the chi in your environment affects you. You see, feng shui is considered both the art and the science of interacting with energy. We have found ways to harness sun and wind energy, and we can use feng shui to understand how to interact with other, subtle natural forces. Knowing what they are and where they may be coming from, or when and why they are here, puts us in a better position to make sound decisions in our lives.

A wise man once said that the human body is like a plant: Given proper care and ideal conditions (good soil, water, and sunlight), a plant will grow and thrive. And the same goes for our body—when we have reached inner balance and aligned ourselves with the energy flow of the earth, we will naturally blossom and attract good luck, flourishing from the universal abundance of joy and success, good health, and strong relationships. Feng shui gives us insight to maximize our full potential and harvest those fruits entirely.

Through feng shui we can create a positive environment to nourish and benefit every aspect of our lives. Its techniques help us find the imbalance of five elements within us and in our environment and then apply remedies to restore balance. The procedure is a bit like detective work: it involves investigating the problem, interpreting data, analyzing the situation, and finding the best ways to deal with what was uncovered. Feng shui remedies must be updated at least annually, because chi is changing and evolving all the time; what works this year in one area of the building may not work again next year—in fact, it may even do some damage. So even a small redecorating project can refresh our lives by revitalizing the energy within a building.

Before making any significant commitments, you need to know everything about yourself, whether it relates to your career or your relationship. When projecting your fortune, you must consider the five types of luck (which we'll go over in a minute) and the time frame, taking into account how they relate to your own chi pattern and how big an impact they will have on your decisions. You can incorporate astrology into feng shui to see how the two systems relate in a particular year, decade, or even longer time span, so you can make some educated predictions about the future. Then you can adjust and adapt to gradual changes, preparing yourself and your loved ones for events that may be approaching.

Ancient scholars believed there are five qualities of luck that influence our lives: the most important is fate, followed by "man luck," feng shui, virtues, and effort. As you can see, feng shui is not at the top of the list, and like fate, it has only a limited effect on us—the impact depends on our karma. A happy and healthy life is thought to have a balance of all five qualities.

Let's explore the five types of luck, which affect our lives in different combinations that ultimately determine who we are. That's why each of is unique.

The first kind of luck comes from fate. Some people believe we can't change our fate—and that's quite true, since it has been predetermined by our karmic deeds from as far back as three lifetimes ago. However, our lives are not a product of fate alone; there are other essential factors, other types of luck, involved in their making. Our DNA contains the genetic code that makes us individual, and it also includes our astral body energy. So let's just say that all our rewards, life missions, punishments, unlearned lessons, or unresolved problems are embedded in our DNA.

Fate does set limits and put certain events in our lives. However, we still hold the greater power: the ability to choose how we want to face them. We can choose how to react to the events, and especially if they are bad, how to face them without getting overwhelmed by our emotions. Learning how not to repeat the same mistake is the real life lesson here. So fate does have strict rules, but they can be broken. You and I can certainly change our fate going forward, since we now have the tools to do so.

Next let's talk about "man-luck," virtue, and effort. You might say we create these kinds of luck ourselves; they are what Neil Peart meant when he said, "Luck is when preparation meets opportunity." How influential are these three kinds of luck, and why do they matter? Well, you may have noticed that "self-created" luck is the focus of the first part of this book. What we think and do now dictates our future, for better or for worse. That same principle enables us to tweak our fate and change our destiny. Let me give you an example. If I were told by the world's greatest fortune-teller that I will live to be older than ninety, I could say he was wrong because my bad habits would surely kill me sooner; thus I would *not* fulfill my given fate. Or, enlightened with knowledge about my true potential for a long life, I could adjust my attitudes and conduct appropriately, and the fortune-teller would have been very accurate in his reading.

Now, I also want to mention environmental luck, whose interconnections and influences can be as small as a group of people or a community or as large as a nation or the world. Environmental luck is much more powerful than luck from an individual because it is comprised of a collective mindset. This kind of luck is impacted by cycles of time and space, i.e., the yearly and monthly cycles of the five elements energy flow interacting with the eight directions. In other words, since we can expect the pattern of night following day and summer following spring, we can get a gleam of the future with the aid of ancient feng shui systems called Loushu Magic Square and the Flying Stars.

Traditional Feng Shui Systems

There are about five or six schools today that teach feng shui, an ancient art that was once a closely guarded secret. The Flying Stars (Feixing) method is the most popular, and that is what we'll be discussing. We'll also incorporate well-known methods from various other schools of teaching. Granted, there may be some disagreement among them, which can cause confusion, but don't be alarmed—once you become familiar with them, you'll be able to decide which method (or combination of methods) is best for you.

The Landform System

Ancient feng shui techniques were plain and simple. They involved nothing more than close observation of the outside environment, but they did require highly advanced skills and intuition in order to correctly interpret the land and weather conditions. These early methods are not as commonly practiced today, especially for lay people, since not everyone is trained in the techniques; nor is it easy to access our intuition for guidance, although feng shui is highly effective when we do. Gill Hall's book *The Practical Encyclopedia of Feng Shui* illustrates the Landform method. The earliest feng shui system ever developed, it was used for locating farmlands, villages, and buildings.

The Compass System

This method, derived from the I Ching system, uses an ancient recording tool called a luo-pan to aid in the interpretation of the land. A luo-pan is a kind of compass inscribed with symbolic meanings of the energies of the universe—the natural orders of heaven, man, and earth. This tool enabled feng shui practitioners to determine what places were suitable for human habitation and how to prosper from the surrounding natural abundance.

We will put our focus on this technique, which in my opinion is the preferred method, since it makes sense that energies must first be located and used as a reference for any assessments, if at all possible. This method is easier to learn than the Landform method, which relies entirely on intuition.

Feng Shui Basics

There are a few key pieces of information you need to get acquainted with before we move on to applying feng shui, and that's what this chapter is all about. We will first become familiar with the yin-yang and five elements principles, because we will use them to either activate the auspicious stars in the sections of our home or diminish those that are harmful. We'll discuss some Chinese astrology, turn our focus to the simple but important Bagua Eight House method, and finally move on to more complex levels of Flying Stars feng shui.

The Yin-Yang Principle

In feng shui, everything has to do with either yin or yang and the five elements principles. The Taoist philosophy of the beginning of life goes something like this: yin and yang forces originated from nothingness, like the binary code in our computing system. Yin and yang gave birth to heaven and earth, and from this dualist principle came the five elements and the forces of chi that made everything in the universe.

YIN	YANG
Earth	Heaven
Moon	Sun
Dark	Light
Night	Day
Female	Male
Water	Mountain
Receptive	Creative
Negative	Positive
Even	Odd
Black	White
Passive	Active
Descending	Ascending
Contract	Expand
Stillness	Movement
Sleep	Awake
Low	High
Landscape	Structure
Cold	Hot
Soft	Hard
Tiger	Dragon

Yin and yang forces are constantly battling each other, each vying for dominance. Due to natural variations in their strength over time, one eventually succeeds and the other yields until the losing force gathers enough strength to take over again—and so the cycle goes. Table above shows these two opposing forces of energy complementing each other: that is the underlying basis for everything that has ever existed. There are two sides to a coin in yin-yang nature, and in human nature there are, as well—a positive and a negative. For example, water and fire generate and sustain life in their positive forms, but they turn deadly in their negative forms (e.g., storms, floods, or wildfire). Wood is not only a vital form in the ecosystem, but it also provides human shelter, and metal supplies shelter and has countless industrial uses, but both wood and metal in their negative forms can be lethal. Earth nurtures countless lives, but it also can take away lives in its negative form by breeding diseases. As for humans, our nature is compassionate and loving, but it also can be depraved when it is controlled by greed and hatred.

Five Forces of Creation: Five Elemental Energies

Feng shui involves the five chi-energy forces that are the source of all things in the universe, including the seven human emotions. These forces are organized into a natural order that begins with Wood, followed by Fire, Earth, Metal, and Water. Feng shui experts have a great understanding of the symbolic meaning of the five elements, as well as their associations. This skill enables them to make highly accurate assessments of a space to guide them toward the right remedies or enhancements for energy balance.

Feng shui uses symbols, characters, images, materials, colors, shapes, aromas, lighting, and sound to encourage energies to interact with us so we will reach our objectives. So it makes sense for us to take the time to familiarize ourselves with the five elements tables, which are essential for investigating possible causes of injury or predicting future events. More important, we must use this information in order to bring energies back into balance. Whether we're working with our bodies or our environment, aligning ourselves to the natural flow of the universe is always beneficial.

WOOD ELEMENT	SYMBOLS, MEANINGS AND ASSOCIATIONS (Table-6a)
Symbolic Meanings	Thunder, shake, new growths, becoming, vitality, life, renew, success.
Energy	Expansive, up and outward.
Climate	Wind
Direction Season Bagua *KUA* Numbers	East, Southeast Spring 3, 4
Shape / Color	Rectangle / green.
Body Anatomy Body System Sense Taste	Liver, gall bladder, spinal cord, nerve, brain, eyes, teeth, legs, feet. Nervous system Sight Sour
Food and Drink	Vegetable, herbs,
Emotion	Anger
Positive Nature Negative Nature	Kindness, generous, energetic, innovative, outgoing. Anger, frustration, greed.
Disease Conditions	Wind related, and/or infatuate with appearances.
Pets	Cats, rabbits.
Industries	Carpentry, herbal, lumber, gardening, nursery, publisher, artist, arts and crafts, art designers, charity, aeronautic, police, astrology, business.
Associations	Forest, trees, plants, tall buildings, posts, document, wooden furniture, sculpture, weaved baskets, books, fabrics, tree scenery images, children, and invention.

FIRE ELEMENT	SYMBOLS, MEANINGS AND ASSOCIATIONS (Table-6b)
Symbolic Meanings	Heat, sun, brightness, spirit, fame, recognition, joy, warmth, awareness.
Energy	All directions, powerful luminosity.
Climate	Heat
Direction Season Bagua KUA Numbers	South Summer 9
Shape / Color	Triangle / red, pink, purple.
Body Anatomy Body System Sense Taste	Heart, small intestine, blood, tongue. Circulatory system Taste Bitter
Emotion	Joy / Love
Positive Nature Negative Nature	Happiness, compassion, passionate, courteous. Impatience, hatred, impulsive, aggressive, short temper, expressive, destructive.
Disease Conditions	Heat and dryness related, and/or addicted to taste.
Pet	Horse
Career Industries	Electronic, chemical, gas/oil energy, electrical engineering, explosive industry, electronic, manufacture, lighting, cooking, restaurants, welding, chemical.
Associations	Fire, sun, candle, light, explosion, electrical, electronic gargets, high pitch roof, fire images, chemicals.

EARTH ELEMENT	SYMBOLS, MEANINGS AND ASSOCIATIONS (Table-6c)
Symbolic Meanings	Womb, nurture, mountain, stability, health, relationships.
Energy	Sideward, central.
Climate	Damp
Direction Season Bagua KUA Numbers	Center, Southwest, Northeast. Last 18 days of every season. 2, 5, 8
Shape / Color	Square / yellow, brown, orange
Body Anatomy Body System Sense Taste	Spleen, stomach, pancreas, muscles, hands, fingers. Digestive system Touch Sweet
Emotion	Worry
Positive Nature Negative Nature	Nourish, openness, acceptance, calm, dependable, loyal, trustful, patience. Obsession, stubborn, loneliness, slow.
Disease Conditions	Wetness related, and/or extreme fond to touch.
Pets	Dogs, birds, tortoises or turtles.
Career Industries	Agriculture, food, mining, real estate, civil engineering, construction, gardening, nursery, glass, cement, research, politic, education, government, laws, and ceramic mfg.
Associations	Land, mountain, boulder, stones statue, structure, quartz crystals, ceramic tile, porcelain, clay, vase, soil, earthquake, and earth related images.

METAL ELEMENT	SYMBOLS, MEANINGS AND ASSOCIATIONS (Table-6d)
Symbolic Meanings	Heaven, sky, strength, unyielding, authority, harvest, transformation, communication.
Energy	Inward, compact.
Climate	Dry
Direction Season Bagua KUA Numbers	West, Northwest. Autumn. 6, 7
Shape / Color	Round, sphere, circle / metallic, white, grey.
Body Anatomy Body System Sense Taste	Lungs, large intestine, head, skin, nose, mouth. Respiratory system. Smell Caustic
Emotion	Grief
Positive Nature Negative Nature	Courage, strength, intuitive, righteousness, leadership, brave, disciplined. Sadness, depression, isolation, inflexible, danger, strike and destructive.
Disease Conditions	Dryness related, and/or addicted to aroma.
Pet	Frog
Career Industries	Precious metal, Jewelry, bank, finance related institutions, investments, stocks trading, credit, money coins, communication, PR, machinery, train, sheet metal shop, auto mechanic and engineering, technician, military, and gun.
Associations	All metals, domes and rounded buildings, metal furnishings, shinny objects, metal coins, statue, ornaments, pots, non-digital clocks, winding music box, wind chimes, metal related images.

WATER ELEMENT	SYMBOLS, MEANINGS AND ASSOCIATIONS (Table-6e)
Symbolic Meanings	Gentleness, nurture, intuitive, life journey, wealth, success.
Energy	Sink, downward flow, lower place, powerful.
Climate	Cold
Direction Season Bagua KUA Numbers	North Winter 1
Shape / Color	Wavy / blue, black.
Body Anatomy Body System Sense Taste	Kidneys, Urinary bladder, bone, ears. Excretory system Hearing Salty
Emotion	Fear
Positive Nature Negative Nature	Gentle, resourceful, amass, supportive, flexible, adaptable, memory, sociable. Exhaustion, anxiety, unstable, loss, intrusion, sensitive, perishing.
Disease Conditions	Coldness related and/or exposed to extreme noises.
Pet	Fish
Industries	Fishing, beverages, import/export, transportation, media, health care, medicine, sex, insurance, human resources, cleaning, water sports, all water related images.
Associations	All water related: Sea, lake, river, pond, well, water fountain, water fall, fish, wavy building shape, mirror, glass, water crystals, bird bath, money, water images.

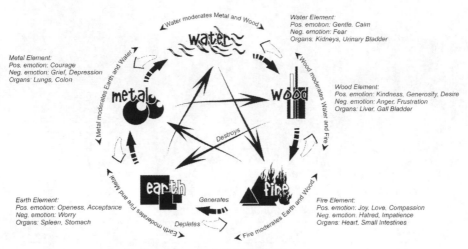

Four Energy Processing Cycles of The Five Elements

Diagram 6.1 *The five elements of the chi (energy) process in feng shui systems. Chinese medicine is based solely on the five elements principle.*

The Principle of Five Elements Cycles

The invisible energy forces (chi) of the five elements are constantly interacting, resulting in four distinct energy cycles: the Generative Cycle, the Depletion Cycle, the Destructive Cycle, and the Moderating Cycle. Traditional Chinese medicine, chi-kung, and tai chi all were born from this powerful principle. Study the four cycles well and you'll see why they are necessary when applying feng shui.

The Generative Cycle: This is a natural cycle used for enhancement. Moving in a clockwise direction, as illustrated in diagram 6.1, Wood gives fuel to Fire; heat creates Earth, which forms Metal; when melted, Metal changes into a liquid state, generating Water; and Water then nourishes Wood.

The Depletion Cycle: We use this cycle as a feng shui cure to exhaust any overwhelming elements. Moving counter-clockwise, Fire consumes Wood, weakening its energy; similarly Wood consumes Water, weakening its energy; too much Water weakens Metal; when Earth is not under pressure it exhausts Metal; and finally, strong Fire exhausts Earth's energy.

The Destructive Cycle: This cycle allows us to control and regulate undesirable elements. Wood cramps Earth with its roots; Earth clogs up Water while naturally destroying Fire; Metal melts under heat, but when cooled to its solid state, it can cut through Wood.

The Moderating Cycle: When the other three cycles aren't good options, this fourth cycle will come in handy. It acts as a moderator between two conflicting elements. For example, if a Fire person must deal with a Water person, then a Wood person would be ideal to call into the discussion because Wood moderates Fire and Water. Fire moderates Earth and Wood; Earth moderates Metal and Fire; Metal moderates Water and Earth; and Water moderates Wood and Metal.

Things to Consider in Your Environment

Rooms

The location of a room in a home or office is important to its occupants. Some feng shui practitioners think the kitchen is the most important room in a home because that's where the main sources of energy enter the house; it's where we prepare food to nourish our bodies. Others believe the bedroom should get top priority over other rooms because that's where the body renews itself and is revitalized while we sleep. This is probably best left up to you. Nevertheless, we should give serious attention to a room's location, layout, and furnishings. In a business, we need to put the staff and customers in the appropriate place according to the natural energy flow. For example, in a retail store you would want to locate the cash registers and accounting office in the Southeast ("wealth") part of the building, while your marketing or communications personnel should be located in the Northwest corner, the "helpful people" area. Of course, the store should be well organized in general and appealing to customers' senses. When feng shui is properly addressed, cash registers will be busy, staff members will be effective and productive, and customers will be satisfied.

The Effects of Shapes, Colors, Lighting, and Materials

There is a whole lot to talk about in these areas alone. Here are some important considerations we often leave out when planning our home or office:

Everything that crosses our senses has a potentially big impact on our feelings and our health, especially when 90 percent of our sensory input comes from our sense of sight. Nature reminds us of the rise and fall of the energy cycle with its seasonal colors. Symbols and images speak to our subconscious, either inspiring us or depleting our energy. So be selective about the paintings or pictures you put in a room.

Shapes are powerful symbols, with simple geometric shapes conveying different energies:

- Circle = life force (chi), oneness, creation, divine, shield
- Square/Rectangle = stability, solid form, success
- Triangle = power, protection, light, energy

Colors play an important role in evoking certain feelings. A room will broadcast certain energies according to its color combinations and contrasts. Color has a subtle influence on our emotions and moods, so make sure to consider its effects in your design. It is good to use colors according to what the Bagua suggests depending on a room's compass orientation. It's even better if the color scheme in the room is in harmony with your favorite colors. When appropriate and necessary, switch to other color schemes to better align the room with current energy fields. Colors convey meaning; they speak to us if we're paying attention. This is what they're saying:

- White = purity, yang, new
- Black = dark, yin, void, emptiness
- Red = strength, passion
- Orange = energy, creativity
- Yellow = well-being
- Green = growth, success
- Blue = peace
- Indigo = intuition
- Violet = wisdom
- Pink = romance, affection
- Brown = stability
- Metallic = joy, purity, good luck

Lighting affects our subconscious perception of one another and our environment. Our perception of the same object changes with a simple change in a light's color, warmth, or method of illumination. For example, candlelight does indeed bring out our romantic side, while fluorescent light likely doesn't have the same effect. Feng shui uses light to enhance the energy in a room; it's a symbolic gesture of brightening up certain areas of our lives.

Materials evoke certain feelings too. The things we touch daily can either appeal to our senses or entirely repulse us. Plan your furnishings, appliances, and even your kitchenware to create a harmonious energy flow as suggested by the Eight House method. In chapter 7 we will talk about your own personal energy type, which four directions suit you best, and which four could drastically reduce your life's potential.

Aromas and Sounds

Aromas and sounds can stimulate and heighten our senses. The smell of certain foods or plants can make us feel good, offend us, or even make us feel sick, by either raising the energy level in the area or polluting it. Do pay close attention to what aromas are in the air, indoors and out, that may have the unintended effect of arousing our emotions or changing our moods. Consider using aromatherapy or essential oils, as discussed in chapter 6, for enhancement. Planting herbs also can help recover stagnant chi in the home or office.

Think about it: the simple sound of a bell can remind each of us of something different in our lives, especially if we associate it with our childhood. Just like smells, which can evoke old memories, sounds also have a special connotation to our hearts. When used appropriately, sound can be a powerful tool for transforming our emotions because it affects us on the subconscious level. Wind chimes, for example, produce a harmonious sound, so they are a great tool for weakening the two annual malicious stars that appear in our home and workplace.

Doors and Windows

The main entrance of a building should get top priority in feng shui, because chi enters the building there, affecting everything inside. Therefore it is ideal to locate the main doors so that they correspond to your four auspicious directions. Other doors and windows of the building are also important because chi flows in and out through them, most notably when inauspicious stars fly into the area one month each year. It's best to keep doors and windows in the affected areas tightly shut for the extent of the stars' stay. Keep an eye on these hostile stars—2, 5, 7, Tai Sui, and

Three Ruins—as they make their way around our homes and businesses annually. Likewise, lucky stars like 1, 6, 8, and 9 may mingle with and influence our own energies.

Water, Trees, Plants, Flowers, and Boulders

Water is the main source of life. It nourishes plants in the physical world as well as in the feng shui five elements theory. Used in certain areas of our home or workplace, it represents wealth and professional success. Knowing how to locate and activate Water energy can generate powerful opportunities in those areas of our lives. You'll learn more about that in the following chapters.

Proper care must be taken when water is used in feng shui. The water element can be either yang or yin, depending on its nature. Consider the following examples: the ocean is yang, while a pond or a lake is yin; a fast-moving waterfall is yang, while a gentle stream is yin. A pond containing fish and water plants is auspicious compared to a lifeless still-water pond. The size and shape of a pond should be proportional to the surrounding area, neither overwhelming nor too small to generate water energy.

Trees and plants have many therapeutic effects on their surroundings. Besides their primary role in the ecosystem, they encourage life-force energy flow for cleansing the environment. On a smaller scale, for example, they make new life and refresh our own personal environment. Their many colors please our eyes as they decorate our fields and gardens, their enticing scents always tempting us to stay longer. They provide shelter and nourishment to countless living species, as well as various spirits, all within the boundaries of our own yard or garden.

Locate indoor and outdoor plants to suit your environment based on the suggestions you get from the Loushu Magic Square (explained in detail in chapter 7). Although they belong to the Wood element, trees and plants can be used to represent other elements by their color, shape, or texture. Pottery, garden ornaments, and outdoor furniture play a big role and can be used to create a harmonious flow of chi and a peaceful feeling in the space. Make sure spiky and prickly plants point away from where you're sitting so they can't send poison arrows (negative energy) toward you. Long, upright plants such as bamboo are commonly used to lift up suppressed energy in a room with a low ceiling or underneath a staircase. Place plants in the corners of a room to promote energy flow, but place them in the hallways to slow rapidly moving energy. Dead and withered plants should be removed, as they produce stagnant chi.

Many tree species, especially pine and oaks, are great for absorbing the negative energy created by emotional stress. Fruit trees are a symbol of abundance; they stimulate wealth chi when kept in the Southeast Wood territory, but they should be avoided in the West and Northwest Metal territories. Trees and tall hedges can be planted so that they create an illusion of hills and boulders, acting as barricades against incoming poison arrows from a nearby T-junction road, sharp roof, or sharp-edged building corner.

A pleasant and inviting garden or yard requires careful planning. Keep in mind that energies associated with the five elements in your garden do matter.

Wood energy:
- green color, rectangular shape
- all trees, plants, and flowers
- a combination of green and colorful lush plants
- sour taste
- tall columns or pillars, wooden deck and furniture
- sound of wood (i.e., bamboo wind chimes)

Fire energy:
- red and purple colors, triangular or pyramid shape
- upright and pointed or triangular plants
- long and pointy or bushy leaves
- bitter taste
- lighting, fire pit

Water energy:
- blue and black colors, rounded or wavy shape
- water plants, blue plants, fruit trees
- salty taste
- blue pottery or blue glass vase
- water or the sound of a waterfall, stream, or fountain

Earth energy:
- yellow, orange, and brown colors; square shape
- yellow plants (e.g., sunflowers, marigolds)
- sweet taste

- rocks, boulders, clay or concrete pottery, statues and ornaments

Metal energy:
- white, silver, and rust colors, domed shape
- dome-shaped trees or shrubs
- thick, round leaves (e.g., money tree)
- caustic taste
- metallic ornaments and structures
- sound of metal (e.g., metal wind chimes, bell)

Chapter 7

Feng Shui Astrology

Bagua

Bagua, which means "eight trigrams," was developed half a century after the writing of the classic Chinese text I Ching ("the Book of Changes") some 3,500 years ago. Bagua is a representation of the principle of all the energies in the universe. Some know it as the truth of heaven and earth; others refer to it as the journey of life. The ancient sage who developed Bagua believed that the formation of the universe related to yin and yang (matter and energy); hence he created the original Eight Primary Trigrams.

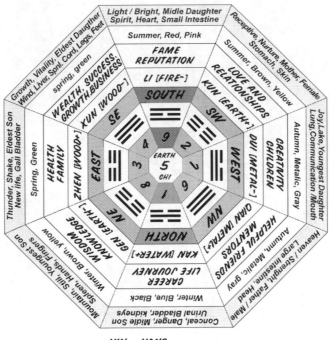

A. The Eight Trigrams Bagua

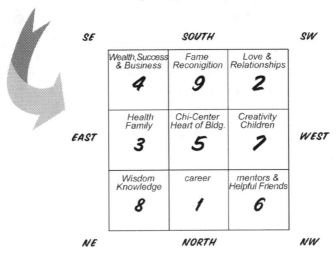

B. The Lou-shu Magic Square

Diagram 7.1a, 7.1b *Bagua arrangement (A), placed north at the bottom, later was translated into three-by-three grids known as the Loushu Magic Square (B).*

Each trigram was made up of three lines, and each line was either solid or broken. Each trigram was assigned the quality of an energy, element, direction, season, and symbolic meaning.

Bagua was originally arranged by King Fu-Hsi in a certain order in an octagonal shape called Early Heaven Bagua; it resembled a turtle shell. The original eight primary trigrams were rearranged and their symbolic meanings expanded about one thousand years later by King Wen, his son, and Confucius—and the result was I Ching's sixty-four hexagrams. Since then the new arrangement, known as the Later Heaven Bagua (illustrated in diagram 7.1a) is widely associated with feng shui, astrology, Chinese medicine, and chi-kung and other martial arts. The Early Heaven Bagua is used today by skilled feng shui masters to identify optimum feng shui burial sites and to facilitate I Ching divination practices.

Feng shui practitioners refer to chi or cosmic forces as "stars." Since chi is an invisible, intangible form of energy that is constantly moving and changing, simple feng shui tools were developed to identify its natural patterns through time and space.

The Bagua serves as the basis for several different feng shui methods: Flying Stars, Three Gates Bagua, the Bazhai Eight Houses, and San-He (Three Compatibility). For best results, try combining various methods in your practice. Don't worry—you will get to know all these methods as we delve deeper into the subject.

Since nothing is static or permanent, feng shui takes into consideration the cyclical nature of change. As some occurrences are likely to repeat over time, the Magic Square was incorporated into the Flying Stars system. The Magic Square is an invaluable tool that is used extensively in feng shui to forecast natural changes that reflect the movement of energy. Practitioners use the Magic Square system to predict future events and map out the energies in a certain area within three common time frames: twenty years, one year, and one month. This is the simplest but most important system used in feng shui.

The Bagua Eight Trigram Symbols and Meanings

Line: Broken, Solid, Broken • Yang Water element • North direction • Kidney, Bladder • Winter season • Black and Blue color • Wavy shape
Represents: Careers
Association: Middle Son
Symbolic Meanings: Moon, Darkness, Concealment, Passion, Trap, Danger

Line: Broken, Broken, Broken •Yang Earth element • Southwest direction • Stomach, Spleen • Late Summer season • Yellow/Brown color • Square shape
Represents: Love and Relationships
Association: Mother, Female
Symbolic Meanings: Earth, Receptiveness, Responsiveness, Submissiveness, Support, Union, Yield

Line: Solid, Broken, Broken •Yang Wood element • East direction • Liver, Gallbladder • Spring season • Green color • Rectangle shape
Represents: Health and Family
Association: Eldest Son
Symbolic Meanings: Thunder, Shaking, New Life Energy, Action and Progression

Line: Broken, Solid, Solid • Yin Wood element • Southeast direction • Late Spring season • Spinal Cord, Nerves, Legs, Feet • Green color • Rectangle shape
Represents: Wealth
Association: Eldest Daughter
Symbolic Meanings: Penetration, Wind, Proceeding Gently, Growth, Vitality, Love romance

Line: None • Earth element • Center sector • Yellow/Brown color • Square shape
Represents: Chi, Center of Life-Force Energy
Symbolic Meanings: Center of Power, Focus, Health, Heart of a Building

Line: Solid, Solid, Solid • Yang Metal element • Northwest direction • Lungs, Large Intestines • Late Autumn season • Metallic/Gray color • Round/Spherical shape
Represents: Mentors/Helpful People
Association: Father, Male, Authority
Symbolic Meanings: Heaven, Initiation, Firmness, Strength, Creativity

Line: Solid, Solid, Broken • Yin Metal element • West direction • Autumn season • Mouth • Metallic/Gray color • Round/Spherical shape
Represents: Joyfulness, Attraction, Children
Association: Youngest Daughter
Symbolic Meanings: Lake, Change, Flexibility, Joy, Communication

Line: Broken, Broken, Solid • Yin Earth element • Northeast direction • Late Winter season • Hands and Fingers • Yellow/Black color • Square shape
Represents: Wisdom and Knowledge
Association: Youngest Son
Symbolic Meanings: Mountain, Stillness, Stability, Meditation, Ending/New Beginning

Line: Solid, Broken, Solid •Yin Fire element • South direction • Summer season • Heart, Small Intestine • Red/Pink color • Triangle shape
Represents: Fame and Reputation
Association: Middle Daughter
Symbolic Meanings: Sun, Fire, Light, Brightness, Self-Illumination, Attachment, Heart or Spirit

The Eight Characters (Bazhi)

The Bazhi is a Chinese astrological system also known as the four pillars of destiny. It is based on the I Ching's sixty-four hexagrams, which may be related to the sixty-four DNA codons for the creation of life. It is important to note that Bazhi reveals only our life potential, what we call destiny; thus it can be changed. Bazhi is based on our birthday: year, month, day, and hour. A birth chart consists of four heavenly stems (elements) and four earthly branches (twelve zodiac animals) that together form the Bazhi. That means each of us has four elements and four animals in our birth chart.

Taoist theory suggests that heaven and earth came together to create man, so these elements and animals have the governing nature of heaven and rule over us. There are ten heavenly stems of the five yin and yang elements. There are twelve earthly branches that reflect our personalities, our character, and the cycles of time—these are the twelve animal symbols in the Chinese zodiac. The combination of one heavenly element and one animal symbol represents one pair of information about an individual. There are eight paired symbols in a complete birth chart, which constitutes one's Bazhi or chi. Because chi is the energy of the subconscious or the spirit, these different combinations of pairs explains why we are all so different from one another: each of us is pursuing different paths at different times. Our character, personality, and emotions affect our decisions, resulting in our unique destiny. However, all areas of our life are interrelated, as suggested by the I Ching and karmic principles; changing any one area will change other areas, as well.

The Magic Square is used to determine what energies are influencing or impacting the people who live or work under the same roof. Meanwhile the Bazhi, Kua, and Eight Direction systems address each of us personally; they are used to determine which five elements and directions are best for enhancing our individual lives. Those remedies may or may not fit the needs of other occupants of the same building.

Example 1
A female born on August 15, 1975, at 10:00 a.m. would have strong Wood influences. Master Zhongxian Wu, author of *The 12 Chinese Animals*, puts greatest emphasis on the birth month, saying it dictates the general direction of your destiny. He suggests that the birth year contains information about the early part of your life, while the birth hour gives you hints about your potential in later life. Use the information provided in this book to help you interpret your own fortune. Pay particularly close attention to symbols that may or may not have compatible relationships or that appear more than once in your Bazhi birth chart. Determine the symbolic meaning of each of your four animal signs contained in your Bazhi from the twelve Chinese animal symbols below, and see if you can piece together information about the direction of your own destiny (e.g., See sample birth chart below).

The Eight Characters (Bazhi Birth Chart)
Birth Year (1975): yearly element + animal = Wood Rabbit
Birth Month (August): monthly element + animal = Wood Monkey
Birth Day (15): daily element + animal = Water Snake
Birth Hour (10:00 a.m.): hourly element + animal = Fire Snake

The Twelve Chinese Animal Symbols' Traits

Rat
Birth Years: 1924, 1936, 1948, 1960, 1972, 1984, 1996, 2008
Birth Month/Time: Dec. 7–Jan. 5; 11:00 p.m.–12:59 a.m.
Symbolic Meanings: renewing, returning
Positive Traits: enduring, eloquent, intuitive, industrious, innovative, sociable, charming, affectionate
Areas Needing Improvement: indecisive, manipulative, vengeful, obstinate, overambitious
Suitable Careers: inventor, marketer, politician, self-employed

Ox
Birth Years: 1925, 1937, 1949, 1961, 1973, 1985, 1997, 2009
Birth Month/Time: Jan. 6–Feb. 4; 1:00–2:59 a.m.
Symbolic Meanings: preserving, confronting
Positive Traits: enduring, reliable, charitable, stable, hard-working, patient, systematic
Areas Needing Improvement: stubborn, inflexible, narrow-minded, not romantic
Suitable Careers: doctor, realtor, politician

Tiger
Birth Years: 1926, 1938, 1950, 1962, 1974, 1986, 1998, 2010
Birth Month/Time: Feb. 4–Mar. 6; 3:00–4:59 a.m.
Symbolic Meanings: great, luxurious
Positive Traits: enthusiastic, vigorous, vigilant, leader, sincere, friendly, graceful
Areas Needing Improvement: short-tempered, uncontrolled anger, reckless, egotistical, impulsive
Suitable Careers: self-employed, writer

Rabbit
Birth Years: 1927, 1939, 1951, 1963, 1975, 1987, 1999, 2011
Month/Time: Mar. 6–Apr. 5; 5:00–6:59 a.m.
Symbolic Meanings: predominate, prosperous
Positive Traits: artistic, intelligent, cautious, calm, sensitive, kind, compassionate
Areas Needing Improvement: moody, self-indulgent, overcautious
Suitable Careers: diplomat, communications, designer, gardener

Dragon
Birth Years: 1928, 1940, 1952, 1964, 1976, 1988, 2000, 2012
Birth Month/Time: Apr. 5–May 6; 7:00–8:59 a.m.
Symbolic Meanings: transforming, freeing
Positive Traits: talented, vigorous, confident, noble, proud, brave, passionate, decisive
Areas Needing Improvement: excessively proud, arrogant, dictatorial, emotional, explosive
Suitable Careers: musician, designer, motivator, politician

Snake
Birth Years: 1929, 1941, 1953, 1965, 1977, 1989, 2001, 2013
Birth Month/Time: May 6–Jun. 6; 9:00–10:59 a.m.
Symbolic Meanings: great wisdom, intuitive
Positive Traits: wise, intuitive, deep thinker, calm, cautious, kind, generous, self-reliant
Areas Needing Improvement: conceited, distrustful, discontent, unpredictable
Suitable Careers: writer, teacher

Horse
Birth Years: 1930, 1940, 1954, 1966, 1978, 1990, 2002, 2014
Birth Month/Time: Jun. 6–Jul. 7; 11:00 a.m.–12:59 p.m.
Symbolic Meanings: success, leading
Positive Traits: witty, active, powerful, successful, open-minded, friendly, popular
Areas Needing Improvement: arrogant, irritable, short-tempered
Suitable Careers: construction, surgeon, politician

Ram
Birth Years: 1931, 1943, 1955, 1967, 1979, 1991, 2003, 2015
Birth Month/Time: Jul. 7–Aug. 8; 1:00–2:59 p.m.
Symbolic Meanings: retreating, hidden
Positive Traits: honorable, intuitive, peaceful, generous, sincere, polite, romantic, calm, artistic
Areas Needing Improvement: pessimistic, worrisome, shy, moody, stubborn
Suitable Careers: artist, actor, designer, writer, self-employed

Monkey
Birth Years: 1932, 1944, 1956, 1968, 1980, 1992, 2004, 2016
Birth Month/Time: Aug. 8–Sep. 8; 3:00–4:59 p.m.
Symbolic Meanings: vigilant, opportunistic
Positive Traits: powerful, skillful leader, intelligent, wit, inventive, confident, charming
Areas Needing Improvement: impatient, vain, deceptive, over-attached
Suitable Careers: leader, administrator, inventor

Rooster
Birth Years: 1933, 1945, 1957, 1969, 1981, 1993, 2005, 2017
Birth Month/Time: Sep. 8–Oct. 8; 5:00–6:59 p.m.
Symbolic Meanings: faithful, affectionate
Positive Traits: organized, confident, efficient, sociable, influential, faithful
Areas Needing Improvement: boastful, critical
Suitable Careers: administrator, manager, counselor

Dog
Birth Years: 1922, 1934, 1946, 1958, 1970, 1982, 1994, 2006
Birth Month/Time: Oct. 8–Nov. 7; 7:00–8:59 p.m.
Symbolic Meanings: loyal, honest
Positive Traits: loyal, honest, cautious, talented, persistent, reliable, great communicator
Areas Needing Improvement: pessimistic, cynical, fretful
Suitable Careers: musician, designer, medical professional

Boar
Birth Years: 1923, 1935, 1947, 1959, 1971, 1983, 1995, 2007
Birth Month/Time: Nov. 7–Dec. 7; 9:00–10:59 p.m.
Symbolic Meanings: relaxating, cautious
Positive Traits: honest, intelligent, noble, calm, patient, trusting, kind, compassionate
Areas Needing Improvement: superficial, insecure, gullible, materialistic, self-indulgent
Suitable Careers: executive officer, teacher, artist

Determining Your Birth Sign in the Chinese Zodiac

Refer to Bagua diagrams 7.1a for symbols and meanings. Diagram 7.2 will give you the animal symbols and elements for your birth year, birth month, and birth hour, but not your birth day, which is not easily calculable. Birth signs do not go by the Chinese New Year, as many people assume; they actually go by the first day of spring, Li-Chun, which can be found in the Chinese lunar calendar and usually falls on February 4 or 5 on the Western (Gregorian solar) calendar. (By the way, I will be referring to the Western calendar throughout this book.) If your birthday happens to fall on February 4 or 5, check your year of birth in the tables below or consult the Chinese almanac to obtain your birth information. Or the quickest way is to visit the Chinese astrology website FortuneAngel.com, which will figure out the Bazhi for you.

Dragon	Snake
1928 Feb-05, 09:16 to 1929 Feb-04, 15:19	1929 Feb-04, 15:20 to 1930 Feb-04, 20:59
1940 Feb-05, 07:07 to 1941 Feb-04, 12:49	1941 Feb-05, 12:49 to 1942 Feb-04, 18:46
1952 Feb-05, 05:00 to 1953 Feb-04, 10:49	1953 Feb-04, 10:50 to 1954 Feb-04, 16:39
1964 Feb-05, 03:07 to 1965 Feb-04, 08:49	1965 Feb-04, 08:50 to 1966 Feb-04, 14:45
1976 Feb-05, 00:44 to 1977 Feb-04, 06:37	1977 Feb-04, 06:38 to 1978 Feb-04, 12:14
1988 Feb-04, 22:53 to 1989 Feb-04, 04:35	1989 Feb-04, 04:36 to 1990 Feb-04, 10:10
2000 Feb-04, 20:32 to 2001 Feb-04, 02:21	2001 Feb-04, 02:22 to 2002 Feb-04, 08:11
2012 Feb-04, 18:22 to 2013 Feb-04, 00:13	2013 Feb-04, 00:13 to 2014 Feb-04, 06:03

Horse	Ram
1930 Feb-04, 21:00 to 1931 Feb-05, 02:41	1931 Feb-05, 02:42 to 1932 Feb-05, 08:26
1940 Feb-04, 18:46 to 1943 Feb-05, 00:45	1943 Feb-04, 00:46 to 1944 Feb-05, 06:22
1954 Feb-04, 16:40 to 1955 Feb-04, 22:18	1955 Feb-04, 22:19 to 1956 Feb-05, 04:10
1966 Feb-04, 14:46 to 1967 Feb-04, 20:24	1967 Feb-04, 20:25 to 1968 Feb-05, 02:17
1978 Feb-04, 12:15 to 1979 Feb-04, 18:13	1979 Feb-04, 18:14 to 1980 Feb-05, 00:11
1990 Feb-04, 10:11 to 1991 Feb-04, 16:19	1991 Feb-04, 16:20 to 1992 Feb-04, 21:53
2002 Feb-04, 08:12 to 2003 Feb-04, 14:02	2003 Feb-04, 14:03 to 2004 Feb-04, 19:51
2014 Feb-04, 06:03 to 2015 Feb-04,11:50	2015 Feb-04, 11:56 to 2016 Feb-04, 17:43

Monkey	Rooster
1932 Feb-05, 08:27 to 1933 Feb-04, 14:55	1933 Feb-04, 14:56 to 1934 Feb-04, 20:04
1944 Feb-05, 06:22 to 1945 Feb-04, 12:19	1945 Feb-04, 12:19 to 1946 Feb-04, 18:11
1956 Feb-05, 04:11 to 1957 Feb-04, 09:58	1957 Feb-04, 09:59 to 1958 Feb-04, 15:56
1968 Feb-05, 02:18 to 1969 Feb-04, 08:09	1969 Feb-04, 08:10 to 1970 Feb-04, 13:33
1980 Feb-05, 00:12 to 1981 Feb-04, 06:01	1981 Feb-04, 06:02 to 1982 Feb-04, 11:52
1992 Feb-04, 21:54 to 1993 Feb-04, 03:40	1993 Feb-04, 03:41 to 1994 Feb-04, 09:30
2004 Feb-04, 19:52 to 2005 Feb-04, 01:29	2005 Feb-04, 01:30 to 2006 Feb-04, 07:23
2016 Feb-04, 17:45 to 2017 Feb-04, 23:31	2017 Feb-03, 23:31 to 2018 Feb-04, 05:55

Dog	Boar
1922 Feb-04, 22:22 to 1923 Feb-05, 03:58	1923 Feb-05, 03:59 to 1924 Feb-05, 09:57
1934 Feb-04, 20:05 to 1935 Feb-05, 02:54	1935 Feb-05, 02:55 to 1936 Feb-05, 07:39
1946 Feb-04, 18:11 to 1947 Feb-04, 23:58	1947 Feb-04, 23:58 to 1948 Feb-05, 05:49
1958 Feb-04, 15:57 to 1959 Feb-04, 21:46	1959 Feb-04, 21:47 to 1960 Feb-05, 03:26
1970 Feb-04, 13:34 to 1971 Feb-04, 19:32	1971 Feb-04, 19:33 to 1972 Feb-05, 01:28
1982 Feb-04, 11:53 to 1983 Feb-04, 17:45	1983 Feb-04, 17:46 to 1984 Feb-04, 23:29
1994 Feb-04, 09:31 to 1995 Feb-04, 15:23	1995 Feb-04, 15:24 to 1996 Feb-04, 21:13
2006 Feb-04, 07:24 to 2007 Feb-04, 13:14	2007 Feb-04, 13:15 to 2008 Feb-04, 19:00

Rat	Ox
1924 Feb-05, 09:58 to 1925 Feb-04, 16:22	1925 Feb-04, 16:23 to 1926 Feb-04, 23:14
1936 Feb-05, 07:40 to 1937 Feb-04, 13:27	1937 Feb-04, 13:28 to 1938 Feb-04, 19:16
1948 Feb-05, 05:49 to 1949 Feb-04, 11:22	1949 Feb-04, 11:22 to 1950 Feb-04, 17:22
1960 Feb-05, 03:27 to 1961 Feb-04, 09:26	1961 Feb-04, 09:27 to 1962 Feb-04, 15:16
1972 Feb-05, 01:29 to 1973 Feb-04, 07:20	1973 Feb-04, 07:21 to 1974 Feb-04, 13:03
1984 Feb-04, 23:30 to 1985 Feb-04, 05:09	1985 Feb-04, 05:10 to 1986 Feb-04, 11:15
1996 Feb-04, 21:14 to 1997 Feb-04, 03:00	1997 Feb-04, 03:01 to 1998 Feb-04, 08:47
2008 Feb-04, 19:01 to 2009 Feb-04, 00:45	2009 Feb-04, 00:46 to 2010 Feb-04, 06:42

Tiger	Rabbit
1926 Feb-04, 23:15 to 1927 Feb-05, 03:34	1927 Feb-05, 03:35 to 1928 Feb-05, 09:16
1938 Feb-04, 19:17 to 1939 Feb-05, 01:22	1939 Feb-05, 01:23 to 1940 Feb-05, 07:07
1950 Feb-04, 17:22 to 1951 Feb-04, 23:12	1951 Feb-04, 23:12 to 1952 Feb-05, 04:59
1962 Feb-04, 15:17 to 1963 Feb-04, 21:08	1963 Feb-04, 21:09 to 1964 Feb-05, 03:06
1974 Feb-04, 13:04 to 1975 Feb-04, 18:52	1975 Feb-04, 18:53 to 1976 Feb-05, 00:43
1986 Feb-04, 11:14 to 1987 Feb-04, 16:51	1987 Feb-04, 16:52 to 1988 Feb-04, 22:52
1998 Feb-04, 08:48 to 1999 Feb-04, 14:22	1999 Feb-04, 14:23 to 2000 Feb-04, 20:31
2010 Feb-04, 06:43 to 2011 Feb-04, 12:38	2011 Feb-04, 12:39 to 2012 Feb-04, 18:30

The San-He (Three Amity) Method:
Three Animal Signs Compatibility

When the energies of the three earthly branches (twelve animal symbols) meet, they attract each other. When they are combined as a group, they're known as san-he, compatible creatures that work as partners, relying on each other for strength and support. It really is a blessing to have these kinds of relationships in your Bazhi birth chart. If you don't, it's always a good idea to have your two compatible animal symbols around for good luck, especially during your unfavorable year.

There are four groups in this unique system of attraction. Animals within the same group make great companions. Referring to the relationship wheel in diagram 7.2, count clockwise beginning with the one next to your animal sign. Every fourth animal symbol is compatible with yours.

Rat (N), Dragon (SE), and Monkey (SW) belong to the Water group; they are powerful and make good leaders. The Metal group also has something in common: Ox (NE), Snake (SE), and Rooster (W) are perseverant individuals, patient and hardworking. Fire group are Tiger (NE), Horse (S), and Dog (NW); they are naturally impulsive, but they honor justice and advocate for humanitarian and other good causes. Rabbit (S), Ram (SW), and Boar (NW) belong to Wood group; they are calm, artistic, and polite, and they are great lovers. Refer to the wheel in diagram 8.8 to see the twenty-four subdivisions indicating the animal's exact directions.

The san-he partners make exceptional soul mates, family members, friends, and coworkers. When your compatible signs show up on the zodiac, consider them in light of your auspicious years, months, or hours. For general luck support, display the san-he symbols in the direction that corresponds to your sign. For example, a Dragon person will want to place a Monkey, Rat, and Dragon in the Southeast. Furthermore, there are also two wealth positions within a building; you will want to place the san-he symbols in those positions to attract money luck. Also make sure to incorporate the group's element to strengthen the effect.

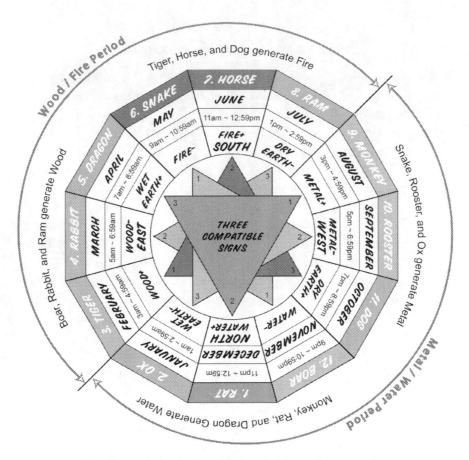

The Three Animal Signs Relationship and Compatibility

Diagram 7.2 *Three compatible animal signs. San-he suggests that when one animal sign's own nature element is combined with that of other animal signs, they form a new, powerful element which can be used to enhance your own personal energy and space. Generally, your best luck comes when your compatible signs show up in the calendar for the year, month, day, or hour.*

Your social and romantic luck are very strong during the compatible year (the year your two san-he animal signs appear on the calendar), meaning you'll have good social and networking opportunities and it will be easy to get along with others. That, in turn, will help you with your career or love life. If you're single, you will have many opportunities to meet or get to know the opposite sex. There's a good chance you will meet someone and fall in love—or you might even get married. The year can put you in a good social mood, so if you're married, your relationship may take a romantic turn. Just make sure not to turn good social luck into a bad romance; instead, use this opportunity to make new friends and build relationships with others in order to enhance your career or bring harmony to your life.

Your compatible years are your time to shine. Don't sit around waiting for opportunities to knock on your door. This could be a good time to put your life plan to work in full force. If you act appropriately, you will be rewarded for your efforts.

Table-7a The 12-Chinese Animal Signs Relationships			
Animal Sign / Year	Orders of Compatibility Excellent | Good	Orders of Incompatibility Severe | Difficult | Moderate | Workable (Animals clashing with Tai Sui)	Make Good working-Partners
1. Rat (2008)	Dragon | Monkey	Horse | Rabbit | Rooster | Ram	Boar | Ox
2. Ox (2009)	Snake | Rooster	Ram | Dragon | Dog | Horse	Rat | Boar
3. Tiger (2010)	Horse | Dog	Monkey | Snake | Boar	Rabbit | Dragon
4. Rabbit (2011)	Ram | Boar	Rooster | Horse | Rat | Dragon	Tiger | Dog
5. Dragon (2012)	Monkey | Rat	Dog | Ram | Ox | Rabbit	Tiger | Rooster
6. Snake (2013)	Rooster | Ox	Boar | Monkey | Tiger	Ram Monkey
7. Horse (2014)	Dog | Tiger	Rat | Rooster | Rabbit | Ox	Snake | Ram
8. Ram (2015)	Boar | Rabbit	Ox | Dog | Dragon | Rat	Horse | Snake
9. Monkey (2016)	Rat | Dragon	Tiger | Boar | Snake	Snake | Rooster | Dog
10. Rooster (2017)	Ox | Snake	Rabbit | Rat | Horse | Dog	Monkey | Dragon
11. Dog (2018)	Tiger | Horse	Dragon | Ox | Ram | Rooster	Rabbit | Monkey
12. Boar (2019)	Rabbit | Ram	Snake | Tiger | Monkey	Tiger | Ox | Rat

When Your Sign Is Incompatible with the Year
The animal signs directly opposite each other on the relationship wheel (diagram 7.2) have an afflictive relationship; they are the least compatible pairings. In general, counting clockwise three spots from your own sign

will give you your second-most unfavorable sign, the ninth spot will be your third-most challenging sign, and the sixth spot—the one opposite yours—is your worst match among all the animals, (e.g., Monkey is incompatible with Boar, Tiger, and Snake, with Tiger being the worst match.)

However, sometimes two conflicting animal signs, like Dragon and Dog, can get along just fine if the elements in their Bazhi are in harmony. Likewise, people in the East and West groups can be good companions if their animal signs have a compatible relationship with one another. (Rabbit and Ram make a good match, as shown on diagram 7.2.) When we take the time to understand someone's personality, we can save ourselves a lot of frustration and senseless expectations. If you're having trouble with a relationship, get to know the person better by studying his or her birth sign and then finding common ground to work with one another. That is what the guiding wisdom of I Ching is about, to live harmoniously with nature and other beings.

Your least favorable year would be one corresponding to your least compatible sign (the spot opposite you on the relationship wheel). It would also be a year when your animal sign is in conflict with the ruling Tai Sui General. During such a year, you'll want to be emotionally prepared and expect the unexpected, since everything you do will seem to hit a brick wall or meet an emotional storm, often out of nowhere. It's also possible that your health may be threatened from illness or injury. So it's worth your trouble to find out how to avoid those problems. As a general rule, the best thing to do is to get lots of rest during the dreadful times. This is your chance for spiritual connection; focus on your own emotional issues. It might be the perfect time to plan your goals or learn new skills to prepare yourself for the future.

One interesting note: our compatibility with others fluctuates. That is, sometimes we tolerate others well, and sometimes we don't. Master Li Kui-Ming suggests that our birth-hour animal sign and the animal sign of the current hour and month can tell us when we are likely to explode if someone pushes our buttons. For example, if you're born in the hours of the Rat, then the Rooster month and hours would be your most intolerant period (or vice versa). Knowing this in advance will help you keep your temper in check.

The following pairs are intolerable with one another: *Rat and Rooster, Ox and Horse, Tiger and Ram, Rabbit and Monkey, Dragon and Boar, Snake and Dog*

The Liu-He (Six Benevolence) Good Luck Charm

A liu-he animal sign on the zodiac could be your lucky charm, especially when you're looking for romance. Two compatible signs on this zodiac share a very special relationship. When they appear in the same year and month, they indicate your best chance of finding a romantic mate because it's considered a favorable year in your social life. Not only will you have many opportunities to meet old and new friends, but you also will be receptive to meeting and talking to people outside your social circle. If you're happily married, use the liu-he sign to help you build relationships in your business or career. Unfortunately, an already shaky relationship may be inclined toward a breakup during this period due to the increased presence of members of the opposite sex.

The liu-he animal friends are as follows: *Rat and Ox; Tiger and Boar; Rabbit and Dog; Dragon and Rooster; Snake and Monkey; Horse and Ram.*

The Yearly Elements

Each year there will be either a yin (-) or yang (+) element of heaven to pair with an earthling animal; together they determine the energetic quality for that year. For example, 2012 was +Water/Dragon, 2013 is –Water/Snake and 2014 will be +Wood/Horse. There are ten elements and twelve animals in all, each pair will repeat over every sixty years. So the next –Water/Snake year will be 2073.

Table-7b Yearly Element and The 12-Animal Signs Element			
New Animal Symbol begins on Feb. 4	Yearly Element	Animal Symbol in Orders of 12-year Cycle	Animal's Nature-Element
2008	+Earth	1. Rat	+Water
2009	–Earth	2. Ox	–Earth
2010	+Metal	3. Tiger	+Wood
2011	–Metal	4. Rabbit	–Wood
2012	+Water	5. Dragon	+Earth
2013	–Water	6. Snake	–Fire
2014	+Wood	7. Horse	+Fire
2015	–Wood	8. Ram	–Earth
2016	+Fire	9. Monkey	+Metal
2017	–Fire	10. Rooster	–Metal
2018	+Earth	11. Dog	+Earth
2019	–Earth	12. Boar	–Water

The Eight House (Bazhai) System:
The Magic in Feng Shui Astrology

Your Principle (Kua) Number and Self-Element

Found under the Eight House system, your life *kua* (or gua) is a very important number to remember. It is the number in the center grid of a Magic Square, representing the star cycle at the time of your birth. In other words, because your chi corresponded with the alignment of heavenly bodies at the moment you were born, it is only natural that your body responds positively to that alignment. When you're in tune with your chi, it is unlikely to disrupt your body's biochemistry. As a result you'll feel happy and healthy, you will have mental clarity, and you won't be overwhelmed by your emotions. Use your life kua information to determine your eight directions of luck for a personalized feng shui that will help you remove blockages and unleash your true potential.

Your kua number also tells you your life element, which is different from your birth year element. Basically, it's considered your lucky element; the goal is to surround yourself with energies that support and align with the energy of your life element. For example, the Generative Cycle relationship from the five elements theory tells us that an Earth Kua-8 person would function best living in the West-group house and driving a yellow or brown car (and not green or gold). Southwest is his or her body's best chi alignment with the earth's energy fields. A Metal Kua-6 person would function best in a career that relates to metal (and not a fire-related business); sleeping and sitting facing west would be beneficial to his or her vital energy field. On the other hand, a Fire Kua-9 person would ideally live and work in the eastern part of the region; facing east or southeast could help speed recovery from health issues, and facing north could help with finding a mate. The kua number is necessary for determining cures or enhancements in a Bagua or Flying Star system, so let's talk about how to find yours.

How to Find Your Life Kua Number

Take the digits of your birth year, add the last two digits, and keep adding until you get a single digit. For example, a male born on March 25, 1993 (Water Rooster year) would add 9 + 3 to get 12, and then in order to get a single digit, he would add those digits: 1 + 2 = 3. A male born before 2000 should subtract that number from 10 to get his kua number: 10 - 3 = 7, so his kua is a 7 Metal. A female with the same birth year would add five to that result: 3 + 5 = 8, so her kua is an 8 Earth. The math is a little different for those born in the year 2000 or later: males subtract the single digit from 9, while females add it to 6.

Therefore, the young man from the example has traits characteristic of both Water and Metal elements combined with Rooster and Rabbit personalities. Refer to table 7c to find your kua, or do your own calculations to get the number.

Table-7c Male (M) and Female (F) Life-KUA (*Kua*) Numbers

YEAR BORN	SYMBOL	YEAR ELEMENT	KUA M	KUA F
1915	RABBIT	WOOD-	4	2
1916	DRAGON	FIRE+	3	3
1917	SNAKE	FIRE-	2	4
1918	HORSE	EARTH+	1	5
1919	RAM	EARTH-	9	6
1920	MONKEY	METAL+	8	7
1921	ROOSTER	METAL-	7	8
1922	DOG	WATER+	6	9
1923	BOAR	WATER-	5	1
1924	RAT	WOOD+	4	2
1925	OX	WOOD-	3	3
1926	TIGER	FIRE+	2	4
1927	RABBIT	FIRE-	1	5
1928	DRAGON	EARTH+	9	6
1929	SNAKE	EARTH-	8	7
1930	HORSE	METAL+	7	8
1931	RAM	METAL-	6	9
1932	MONKEY	WATER+	5	1
1933	ROOSTER	WATER-	4	2
1934	DOG	WOOD+	3	3
1935	BOAR	WOOD-	2	4
1936	RAT	FIRE+	1	5
1937	OX	FIRE-	9	6
1938	TIGER	EARTH+	8	7
1939	RABBIT	EARTH-	7	8
1940	DRAGON	METAL+	4	2
1941	SNAKE	METAL-	3	3
1942	HORSE	WATER+	2	4
1943	RAM	WATER-	1	5
1944	MONKEY	WOOD+	9	6
1945	ROOSTER	WOOD-	8	7
1946	DOG	FIRE+	7	8
1947	BOAR	FIRE-	6	9
1948	RAT	EARTH+	5	1
1949	OX	EARTH-	4	2
1950	TIGER	METAL+	3	3
1951	RABBIT	METAL-	2	4
1952	DRAGON	WATER+	1	5
1953	SNAKE	WATER-	9	6
1954	HORSE	WOOD+	8	7
1955	RAM	WOOD-	7	8
1956	MONKEY	FIRE+	6	9
1957	ROOSTER	FIRE-	5	1
1958	DOG	EARTH+	4	2
1959	BOAR	EARTH-	3	3
1960	RAT	METAL+	2	4
1961	OX	METAL-	1	5
1962	TIGER	WATER+	9	6
1963	RABBIT	WATER-	8	7
1964	DRAGON	WOOD+	7	8
1965	SNAKE	WOOD-	6	9
1966	HORSE	FIRE+	5	1
1967	RAM	FIRE-	4	2
1968	MONKEY	EARTH+	3	3
1969	ROOSTER	EARTH-	2	4
1970	DOG	METAL+	1	5
1971	BOAR	METAL-	9	6
1972	RAT	WATER+	8	7
1973	OX	WATER-	7	8
1974	TIGER	WOOD+	6	9
1975	RABBIT	WOOD-	5	1
1976	DRAGON	FIRE+	4	2
1977	SNAKE	FIRE-	3	3
1978	HORSE	EARTH+	2	4
1979	RAM	EARTH-	1	5
1980	MONKEY	METAL+	9	6
1981	ROOSTER	METAL-	8	7
1982	DOG	WATER+	7	8
1983	BOAR	WATER-	6	9
1984	RAT	WOOD+	5	1
1985	OX	WOOD-	4	2
1986	TIGER	FIRE+	3	3
1987	RABBIT	FIRE-	2	4
1988	DRAGON	EARTH+	1	5
1989	SNAKE	EARTH-	9	6
1990	HORSE	METAL+	1	5
1991	RAM	METAL-	9	6
1992	MONKEY	WATER+	8	7
1993	ROOSTER	WATER-	7	8
1994	DOG	WOOD+	6	9
1995	BOAR	WOOD-	5	1
1996	RAT	FIRE+	4	2
1997	OX	FIRE-	3	3
1998	TIGER	EARTH+	2	4
1999	RABBIT	EARTH-	1	5
2000	DRAGON	METAL+	9	6
2001	SNAKE	METAL-	8	7
2002	HORSE	WATER+	7	8
2003	RAM	WATER-	6	9
2004	MONKEY	WOOD+	5	1
2005	ROOSTER	WOOD-	4	2
2006	DOG	FIRE+	3	3
2007	BOAR	FIRE-	2	4
2008	RAT	EARTH+	1	5
2009	OX	EARTH-	9	6
2010	TIGER	METAL+	8	7
2011	RABBIT	METAL-	7	8
2012	DRAGON	WATER+	6	9
2013	SNAKE	WATER-	5	1
2014	HORSE	WOOD+	4	2

The East and West Groups

The kua are divided into two groups of people, the East and West. These two groups tend to conflict with one another due to their elemental differences, so they should not be mixed together. In general, east-sitting houses will benefit folks in the East group, while west-sitting house will suit those in the West group.

East Group
Kua & Trigram name (building type): 1-Kan, 3-Zhen, 4-Xun, 9-Li
Direction: North, East, Southeast, South

West Group
Kua & Trigram name (building type): 2-Kun, 5-Chi, 6-Qian, 7-Dui, 8-Gen
Direction: Southwest, Center, Northwest, West, Northeast

How the Eight House Theory Can Change Your Luck

If your building's exterior or physical conditions are not suitable for you but they are out of your control, don't give up hope. There is one powerful yet unbelievably simple way to change your luck very dramatically: tap into your personal auspicious directions. Just like a cell phone, you're at your weakest when you're out of alignment with your energy source. When you're being hit with a stream of bad luck, it's best to find a stronger signal: tune into the Eight House theory to help you make simple adjustments. The goal is to orient yourself so the natural flow of chi along your body's meridians corresponds to the earth's magnetic fields. Again, the logic behind this is that the earth's energy fields influence our body's system for controlling hormones—that is, the tiny pituitary and pineal glands located deep inside our brains, which affect our moods and emotions and lead us to think or behave in certain ways. We know now that unbalanced brain chemistry eventually leads to unhealthy lifestyles with hazardous consequences.

Table-7d The Eight-House Theory: Eight Directions of Luck

Kua / Trigram	Building's Energy Field			Four Auspicious Facing Directions				Four Inauspicious Facing Directions			
	Building's Sitting Direction	Element	Group	1st Main Wealth	2nd	3rd Secondary Wealth	4th	5th	6th	7th	8th
1 / Kan	N	+Water	East	SE	E	S	N	W	NE	NW	SW
2 / Kun	SW	+Earth	West	NE	W	NW	SW	E	SE	S	N
3 / Zhen	E	+Wood	East	S	N	SE	E	SW	NW	NE	W
4 / Xun	SE	-Wood	East	N	S	E	SE	NW	SW	W	NE
5 / Chi	West group female Kua 5 (Earth) change to a 2 (Earth, Kun)										
	West group male Kua 5 (Earth) change to a 8 (Earth, Gen)										
6 / Qian	NW	+Metal	West	W	NE	SW	NW	SE	E	N	S
7 / Dui	W	-Metal	West	NW	SW	NE	W	N	S	SE	E
8 / Gen	NE	-Earth	West	SW	NW	W	NE	S	N	E	SE
9 / Li	S	-Fire	East	E	SE	N	S	NE	N	SW	NW

Key: N=North S=South E=East W=West NE=Northeast NW=Northwest SE= Southeast SW=Southwest

The Eight House method gives your eight personal directions for positioning your home, bed, or desk. They may be different than those of other people around you, so work out the best possible options for everyone living or working under the same roof. Table 7d shows your four good and four bad directions. Depending on which ones are available and which are more important to you at the moment, orient yourself to sit facing or sleep with your head pointing to any of your good directions, and you'll benefit from its influences.

If you and your partner are in opposite groups but share a bed, either of you can reposition yourself slightly so your head points toward the direction of your animal birth sign (thus attracting its benefits). Suppose, for example, that a West-group Kua-6 Metal Ram man shares a south-facing bed with an East-group Kua-3 Wood Dog woman. Since Fire from the south will destroy Metal, then it would be better for the man to simply adjust his sleeping position so his head points toward a southwest-a (SW-a) Ram direction. (Refer to diagram 8.8, the twenty-four subdivision wheel, for a directional illustration.) Or if the headboard faces west, the woman could shift so her head points toward a Dog direction in northwest-a (NW-a).

The Eight Directions' Attributes

The first four directions belong to the same element group, bringing good health, joy, and happiness into your life. But avoid the last four directions, which could bring not only bad luck, but poor health resulting in chaos. In the context of relationships, when a couple's kua numbers are compatible, like 1 and 6 according to the Generative Cycle (Metal generates Water), their lives will flourish. But a couple with kua numbers 3 and 6 will have an unharmonious relationship, because this pair belonging to the Destructive Cycle (Metal destroys Wood).

Before you settle on using any directions, even when they're good, it's wise to yield to a few annual hostile stars. If you're recovering from an injury and your Tian Yi Second direction is inflicted with either a (sickness) star 2 or (accident) star 5, then your First direction is your next-best choice. If you run out of better options, settle on the ones that are least harmful.

It would be ideal to have the main doors to your home or office facing your good directions, but if the secondary doors are better oriented for you, by all means use them and avoid the main doors.

First direction: **Sheng Qi—vitality and harmony, life-generating; main wealth position**

First direction is always the most ideal orientation for sleeping (head pointing in that direction) or for placement of your house or desk. It is also the perfect location for your master bedroom and main door. The Eight House theory points to this as your main wealth direction.

Second direction: **Tian Yi—celestial doctor, health**

Second direction is good for replenishing vital health, especially when you're feeling ill or in recovery.

Third direction: **Yan Nian—extended years (longevity), relationships; secondary wealth position**

Third direction is about building good relationships. It's perfect for orienting the bed in order to initiate harmony in the family. It's also auspicious to face that direction when you're seeking a mate or looking for a friend to lend a hand; facing that way also encourages longevity. This is an alternative wealth position according to Eight House theory.

Fourth direction: **Fu Wei—lying down, growth**

Fourth direction is related to subtle healing energy. It's great for revitalizing our body's chi and for boosting mental clarity. Tap into this direction for the office or study room. It's good for children's rooms to face this direction to help with their academic development, school projects, and exams.

Fifth direction: **Huo Hai—mishaps, injury**

Fifth direction is associated with obstacles abroad and feelings of terror caused by frightening and sad events.

Sixth direction: **Wu Gui—five ghosts**

Sixth direction creates severe disharmony and bickering. It's definitely an area to avoid during family gathering or meetings if most members are in different East/West group.

Seventh direction: **Liu Sha—six killing**
Seventh direction can bring about health and legal problems, fraud, burglary, or robbery. Do not keep your money in this area.

Eighth direction: **Jue Ming—life loss, threatening**
Eighth direction, as the name implies, is the deadliest direction in which to position yourself—literally. It corresponds to the Conflictive Cycle of the five elements theory.

Know Your Lucky Cycles

In the twelve time cycles represented by the twelve Chinese animal symbols, we are naturally affected by the cycles' relationship with our own birth signs (Ba Zhi), and we're also influenced by the elements associated with those cycles. There are two dominant groups of elements in the cycles: Wood-Fire and Metal-Water. The two groups are found in hourly, daily, monthly, and yearly time frames. Generally we have better luck and our lives are smoother if our kua numbers are in harmony with the current cycle, or if we avoid cycles that are not supportive of our lucky element. It's always a good idea to plan your next big project or important event in accordance with your good cycles.

Table-7e Energetic Cycles of Time							
Wood-Fire Predominant Season Spring and Summer				Metal-Water Predominant Season Autumn and Winter			
Tiger (wood)	February 4	1998, 2010	3 am ~ 4:59 am	Monkey (metal)	August 8	2004, 2016	3 pm ~ 4:59 pm
Rabbit (wood)	March 6	1999, 2011	5 am ~ 6:59 am	Rooster (metal)	September 8	2005, 2017	5 pm ~ 6:59 pm
Dragon (earth)	April 5	2000, 2012	7 am ~ 8:59 am	Dog (earth)	October 8	2006, 2018	7 pm ~ 8:59 pm
Snake (fire)	May 6	2001, 2013	9am ~ 10:59am	Boar, water	November 7	2007, 2019	9 am ~ 10:59 am
Horse, fire	June 6	2002, 2014	11am ~ 12:59pm	Rat, water	December 7	2008, 2020	11 pm ~ 12:59 am
Ram, earth	July 7	2003, 2015	1 am ~ 2:59 pm	Ox, earth	January 6	2009, 2021	1 am ~ 2:59 am

To find out what your overall luck would be like during a certain time of day or a certain year, or over the next twelve years, you need to break the time frame down into two half-cycles. That's because animals in the first half of the zodiac are predominantly associated with Wood-Fire elements, while animals in the last half are associated with Metal-Water elements. Thus, East group people with kua numbers 1, 3, 4, or 9 thrive in spring and summer and have declining luck in autumn and winter. On the other hand, West group folks with kua numbers 2, 5, 6, 7, or 8 get their fair share of good fortune in the autumn and winter and then back down in spring and summer. So plan your future projects and events wisely: it's best if your "harvesting" period falls during your lucky cycle so you'll get the most out of your potential.

What Are Your Lucky Foods?

The right foods and beverages can bring you good luck along with good health. For example, Master Li suggests that a woman can increase her odds of meeting a romantic mate if she eats crab, while a man can do the same by eating shrimp. Li divides people into four groups according to the main element missing in their Ba-Zhi (birth chart); this is considered their lucky element.

Participating in activities and eating foods and drinks associated with the element you're lacking can bring your chi into balance. You will also do very well in careers associated with your lucky element. Look at the list below to find out what foods give you better luck.

Birthday: Feb. 19–May 4
Energy Deficiency/Lucky Element: Metal
Avoid: fire-related activities
Lucky Food: beef, frozen food and drink, milk, cheese, ice cream
Suitable Careers: jewelry industry, finance, banking, medical, hotel

Birthday: May 5–Aug. 7
Energy Deficiency/Lucky Element: Water
Avoid: fire-related activities
Lucky Food: fruits, fruit juices, cold food, seafood, tofu, beef, vegetables such as squash
Suitable Careers: marine industry, insurance

Birthday: Aug. 8–Nov. 7
Energy Deficiency/Lucky Element: Wood
Avoid: metal-related activities
Lucky Food: green leafy vegetables, fruit, pork, liver, poultry
Suitable Careers: lumber industry, publishing, journal industry

Birthday: Nov. 8–Feb. 18
Energy Deficiency/Lucky Element: Fire
Avoid: water-related activities
Lucky Food: warm food, lamb chops, eggs, curry, red chili, oatmeal, coffee, chocolate, red wine
Suitable Careers: electronics industry, auto industry, restaurant industry, real estate

NORTH

Diagram 8.1 *A Magic Square is superimposed onto a floor plan layout for locating energy in the house. The same grid can be used to lay out a room or even a desk. In its original form, the sum of the grids of a Magic Square adds up to fifteen in any direction.*

Chapter 8

Applying Feng Shui Systems

The Bagua Feng Shui

The Loushu Bagua serves as the basis for feng shui principles, providing the starting steps for feng shui planning. In fact, it may be all you need to get delightful results. It's fairly straightforward and easy to learn, and it can be applied to any space you want to make changes in the energy.

We will be learning the Flying Star method, and we'll use a compass to find out our facing and sitting directions instead of the luo-pan traditionally used by feng shui practitioners. This information has been transcribed onto charts, tables, and diagrams, so we will need only to find the exact orientation of a building or a room in order to construct the map. For ease of language, I may refer to a house, room, or office as a "building" or "space."

The direction in which a space is facing is one of the most critical pieces of information needed to map out its energy. Because everything else is based on this information, it's imperative that you get it right.

Determining which side of your building is in the "facing" direction can be difficult if the building is located on a corner or if it has an obscure configuration. If you have a clear and simple building configuration, that's terrific, but many folks have a nightmare of a time figuring it out. If you have this problem, take the advice of Master Lillian Too, author of *Flying Star Feng Shui Made Easy*. She tells her readers to use their best judgment—guided, perhaps, by their intuition. Trial and error is the best way to deal with any uncertainty. As a general rule, she says, the side of a building that has the most activity (people, traffic, noise, light) would be the best choice as the "facing" direction; the "sitting" direction is directly opposite it. For example, the front doors of the house in diagram 8.1 are located in the "career" sector, the North facing direction, while the "fame and recognition" sector is in the South sitting direction.

One challenging problem is that the front doors of some homes are not located on the same side as the facing direction—not the ideal arrangement, but not necessarily unfavorable either. In this case, the facing direction takes precedence over the location of the front doors if the front side of the house faces a busy street.

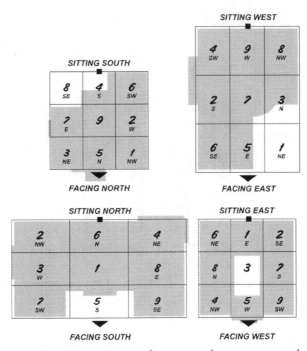

Diagram 8.2 *A Magic Square layout can be superimposed onto any floor plan for locating energies within the building.*

Once you have decided on the facing and sitting directions of a building, superimpose the Magic Square layout over the main part of your floor plans, stretching the grid to cover the length of the building up to nine floors if you have more than one story building.

Diagram 8.2 shows different layouts based on the building's orientation, with the numbers that correspond to the Bagua. It's a bit tricky to deal with buildings that are not square/rectangular shapes. Buildings that have irregular shapes (e.g. an L-shape) will result in sections that either protrude or recess, as illustrated in diagram 8.2, which shows different building configurations. If a protruding section is more than 50 percent of the building's width, there will be missing space (negative space). If a recessed space is less than 50 percent of the building's width, consider it as you would a protruding space (positive space).

Negative space is associated with a lack or something missing, and with difficulty and less auspicious luck. Protruding space means excessiveness, greed, and over controlling behavior. You can correct negative space by placing some features in the missing sector of a building to symbolize completeness.

The Flying Stars System: Loushu Magic Square

Time is a critical factor in feng shui. In this chapter we will apply that factor into our analysis using Flying Stars. Part of the art of achieving balanced chi in the assessed space is understanding the cycles of energy movement as time moves forward. Our goal is to maintain balanced energy in the space being investigated. Yin and yang, the Bagua, and the five elements principle are tools we can use in the process. When applied to the system, they help us understand the quality of energies by revealing their symbolic meanings, patterns, and conditions. That allows us to predict possible future events.

The Flying Stars method uses the Loushu Magic Square arrangement to determine chi movement. Diagram 8.3 illustrates a series of flying stars patterns beginning with #5 star briefly occupying the center sector in 2004 and then proceeding forward in a fixed path of travel and stops. There are nine patterns in one complete cycle, so #5 will be back in the center again in 2013. Numbered patterns in the grids can fly in either forward or reverse order in the sitting and facing stars charts.

Example:
Forward (ascending) order: 5, 6, 7, 8, 9, 1, 2, 3, 4, 5 …
Reverse (descending) order: 5, 4, 3, 2, 1, 9, 8, 7, 6, 5 …

The Magic Square: How to Construct a Yearly Flying Stars Chart

Energies are always moving as time moves forward, so the Magic Square was introduced to keep track of their movements. It is a nine-square (three-by-three) grid representing the numerical and mathematical feng shui system used to study the quality of chi in all eight directions. Each grid or sector will be visited by another number that may or may not be in conflict with other numbers residing in the same sector. (That is, you'll have a yearly and monthly number sharing the same sector.) This is where your skills come into play, because you must analyze the numbered star combinations.

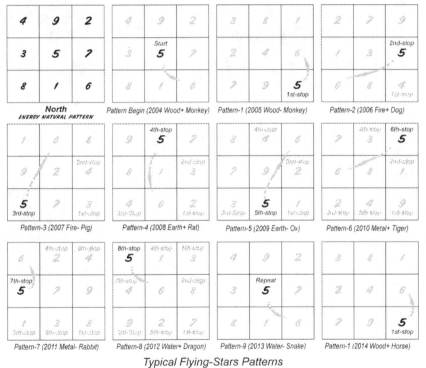

Typical Flying-Stars Patterns

Diagram 8.3 *The Flying Stars system adds a time dimension into the infinite cycle, taking into consideration chi's constant movement. The diagram shows how chi travels from 2004 to 2014 in a fixed path.*

You can find the yearly main stars (numbers) from the Chinese almanac, or refer to table 8a, which indicates which main number takes center grid for the year, as well as the ruling animal. Diagram 8.3 shows the yearly pattern of #5 star's movements in conjunction with other numbers from one sector to the next. These energy movements are the basis for practicing Flying Stars feng shui, so before we move on, familiarize yourself with them.

A typical flying pattern goes like this: start at the center and then move to Northwest, West, Northeast, South, North, Southwest, East, and finally Southeast. Repeat starting from the center.

Table-8a Yearly Main-Star			
Main Number (Center Grid)	Year / Animal	Main Number (Center Grid)	Year / Animal
5	2004 / Monkey	8	2010 / Tiger
4	2005 / Rooster	7	2011 / Rabbit
3	2006 / Dog	6	2012 / Dragon
2	2007 / Boar	5	2013 / Snake
1	2008 / Rat	4	2014 / Horse
9	2009 / Ox	3	2015 / Ram

The Nine Cycles of Chi

The Flying Stars system organizes time into three tiers: upper, middle, and lower cycles. Each tier consists of three 20-year periods or a 60-year revolution, totaling 180 years to complete all three tiers. The Eighth Period is currently in the lower tier. One thing to keep in mind is that every new cycle begins on Li-Chun, which usually falls on February 4 or 5.

The change in strength of a star's energy will have an impact on the sector. For example, #8 star appearing in the center grid is active during the current period, hence that sector is filled with huang-qi, vigorous and vital strength,

Table-8b The Nine (20 years) Periods Cycles	
Year Range (February-4 marks switchover cycle)	Period Number (Appeared at center of grid)
1884 to 1903	2
1904 to 1923	3
1924 to 1943	4
1943 to 1963	5
1964 to 1983	6
1984 to 2003	7
2004 to 2023	8
2024 to 2043	9
2044 to 2063	1

because #8 star denotes powerful and most auspicious energy. Meanwhile, #9 star is progressing with sheng-qi, gathering strength to become the next powerful star in the coming years. Both are valued fortune stars, so feng shui should be activated to stimulate their powers. On the inauspicious side, there's #7, which was a vibrant star very recently. It did bring prosperity to the world, but it is now declining in strength and thus retreating. Since then it has become a violent star, bringing loss wherever it goes, so it must be suppressed using the Depletion Cycle. The nine cycles principle is very important when determining whether a building is carrying good or bad feng shui.

6 *Retreating*	2	4
5	7 *Vigor*	9
1	3	8 *Progressing*

North

7th Period (1984 ~ 2003)
Past period

⑦ *Retreating*	3	5
6	⑧ *Vigor*	1
2	4	⑨ *Progressing*

North

8th Period (2044 ~ 2023)
Current period

8 *Retreating*	4	6
7	9 *Vigor*	2
3	5	1 *Progressing*

North

9th Period (2024 ~ 2043)
Future period

• *February-4th marks the switch-over to the next period cycle.*

Diagram 8.4 *Chi moves forward as time elapses. There are nine energy cycles covering a span of 180 years. Each star is represented by a number that remains in its temporary residence for twenty years. A star indicates what the quality of energy will be for that sector during its stay. When a star becomes a main star (in the center sector), it is charged with high energy and becomes the highlight of the space during its active cycle.*

Have you ever noticed that some buildings just don't seem to perk up, no matter who moves in? When a building brings endless bad luck to the occupants of the home or business, the first thing a feng shui practitioner might look into is the building's state of health, so of speak. The quality of a building's feng shui chi is directly related to its construction year, which falls into one of nine periods. For example, a building constructed between 2004 and 2023 is considered an Eighth Period building; its occupants will benefit from the good feng shui influences dominating the time of its construction. A building constructed in Period 2, 3, 5, or 6 may not have optimum feng shui, because it's suffering from si-qi, dead energy. An extensive renovation can revitalize the energies of an older building, making them harmonious with the current energy field; hence it will be renewed. That means we can turn a Seventh Period or First Period building into a prime, Eighth Period building. Now that is one powerful tool you should keep in mind!

Well, we've learned all the feng shui tools that can give us an outlook on the future. Knowing in advance the cycles of upcoming energies and their associations allows us to make plans for the future and perhaps avoid unpleasant situations

In order to see what careers will be trending going forward, we need to look at the twenty-year cycle. Trending careers in the Seventh Period (1984–2003) involved the use of "mouth," according to Master Li (see diagram 7.1a). It's likely that someone whose career involved the mouth, such as singing, would have done remarkably well. Li predicts that in the Eighth Period, the "hands" will be the next career trend. The Seventh Period ended on February 3, 2004, and since the end of that cycle, the retreating star, #7, has become vicious, bringing loss, robbery, and fraud. If you pay attention, you'll notice that careers are over for many legendary singers as they disappear from our lives. One reason is that the #7 star is associated with loss related to the mouth.

So here we are, already nine years into the Eighth Period (2004–2023). The yin earth #8 star takes the spotlight, which means its energy is in its prime. According to Bagua, the number eight denotes wisdom, stillness, and youngest son, and it is associated with hands and fingers. Maybe that explains why tattoo parlors, nail salons, and foot-massage businesses have been booming in your town since the beginning of this decade. So what's the next career choice or business after eight? It is number nine, of course, and it has something to do with the "heart."

The Magic Square: How to Construct the Monthly Flying Stars Charts

A monthly Flying Stars chart is the same as an annual chart. The one number you will need to begin charting is the main or "center" number, and the rest follows the typical flying pattern. The new patterns begin on February 4 of every year, and so I use the fourth as my switchover day for every month. But if you want to be technical, mark the dates below on your calendar to make the monthly switchover:

February 4 (Tiger), March 6 (Rabbit), April 5 (Dragon), May 6 (Snake), June 6 (Horse), July 7 (Ram), August 8 (Monkey), September 8 (Rooster), October 8 (Dog), November 7 (Boar), December 7 (Rat), and January 6 (Ox)

Table-8c: Monthly Main-Star Chart			
Main Number (Appears at Center of Grid)	Year Begin	Animal Year Symbols	Four Relationships
8	February 4	Rabbit, Horse, Rooster, Rat	Four Directions
5	February 4	Ox, Dragon, Ram, Dog	Four Earth
2	February 4	Monkey, Snake, Tiger, Boar	Four Corners

Look for the animal year from table 8c. Put the main number (left column) in the center grid of your Magic Square, then plot in eight other numbers in their places as illustrated in the Flying Stars pattern. For example, #8 resides in the center grid for Rabbit year on February 4, 2011, moves to Northwest on March 6, and ends with #6 in the center grid on January 6, 2011; #5 will then take the center grid on February 4, 2012, for Dragon year; #2 will take the spotlight for the month in a Snake year on February 4, 2013, and then moves on to the next stop, and so on.

Symbolic Meanings of the Nine Stars

When reading the feng shui map of your property from the superimposed Magic Square layout, pay attention to the group of stars (numbers) that reside in the same sector, especially their strengths and how their elements relate to each other and to that of the sector. Now bear in mind that those stars could be in any combination, so a thorough analysis is important.

Feng shui refers to the quality of chi as "stars" that are represented by nine numbers as ascribed in the Bagua symbols. Each star has its own unique qualities and strengths that can impact our emotions, moods, thoughts, and health. In the current period, #1, #6, #8, and #9 stars are referred to as fortunate white stars that should be activated to exploit their maximum influences. On the other hand, pay close attention to #2 and #5 stars for their brute force, which needs to be constrained. The #3 and #7 stars exert their dreadful energies by creating challenging situations for victims. When a star joins forces with another numbered star, they both either double their strength or manifest into something else entirely as suggested by the I Ching principle. Use your knowledge of the yin-yang theory, the five elements theory, symbols, affirmations, and the stars' inherent meanings (shown below) to help you make an accurate analysis. It's helpful to know what stars mean when applying enhancements or remedies.

The following He-Tu astrology star pairings are regarded as exceptionally auspicious whenever they (heaven and earth) come together to create harmonious order. They may even cancel out the negative effects of other stars. They are 1 and 6; 2 and 7; 3 and 8; and 4 and 9. When the sum of two stars' numbers equals ten, that is also considered auspicious: 2 and 8; 1 and 9; and 6 and 4 make excellent pairs.

Star #1 (Water)
This lucky #1 white star brings substantial fortune and prosperity—career advancement, luck with financial speculation, and romantic developments are its greatest influences. It is auspicious when joined with stars 1, 4, 6, 8, or 9. North, East, and Southeast are filled with fabulous opportunities when visited by #1 star. In He-Tu astrology, the pairings of 1 with 6 and 1 with 9 bring great success and financial and career growth. Star #1 brings academic success and romantic opportunities when combined with #4 in East and Southeast. Meanwhile, financial income increases the most when #1 joins forces with the auspicious #8 star. Traditional feng shui uses Water and Metal to stimulate its power. Star # 1 resides in the North in 2013.

Star #2 (Earth)
The terrifying #2 black star brings sickness, disease, or fatal incidents to the occupants of a space; it is especially harmful to females. Avoid this sector if you are currently ill or in the process of recovering. Your next best option is not to sit facing or sleep with your head pointing in this direction. All stars can become destructive when infused with the energy of this star, but the most deadly pairings are with #2 or #5, which could cloud your judgment, making you vulnerable to mistakes. Meanwhile, the less extreme pairings with #3 or #7 will create misunderstandings that cause fights leading to

losses and injuries. Use Metal to weaken this star's malicious effects—traditional feng shui recommends displaying something like eight ancient coins on a red string, metal wind chimes, or a brass pagoda. Objects that make the sound of metal will work best: wind chimes or a hanging bell, or a piano or music box. Star #2 resides in the Southwest in 2013.

Star #3 (Wood)

#3 jade is a peevish, odd star that can cloud our judgment, causing all kinds of disharmony like resentment, misunderstandings, ugly rumors, bickering, and full-blown arguments. It also tends to aggravate matters that result in legal issues or run-ins with the law. Furthermore, #3 star causes belligerent behavior, including friction with authority. You can expect bitter fights and legal trouble when #3 is infused with the energy of stars 1, 2, 3, 4, 5, 7, or 9 in any sector. It's best to avoid breaking ground in its direction during the year, but if you must break ground, start with adjacent sides first, and then move toward the afflicted section of the property. Apply Fire to exhaust its energy. Traditional feng shui cures recommend placement of red or pink colors, candles, or an incense burner. Jade star #3 resides in the East in 2013.

Star #4 (Wood)

The #4 green star oversees the advancement of scholarly activities, benefiting the world of fine arts and literature. It is associated with academic achievement or education in general. Activate this star with Water element for success with academic or professional exams. If its energies are properly enhanced, students of all ages will benefit from this magnificent star. Those in a quest for nobility or romance should note its annual and monthly position. When infused with stars 1, 4, and 9 in the North, East, and Southeast, there's no limit to the amount of success it can bring. However, combining #4 with negative stars can change its power, threatening health and relationships. The #4 star resides in the Southeast in 2013.

Star #5 (Earth element)

This earth star, also known as #5 yellow, resembles its evil accomplice #2 star but brings even deadlier consequences wherever it lands. In general, this angry star carries with it all sorts of setbacks: unfortunate events, failures, illnesses, and perhaps even death. When joined with any of the nine stars it will surely bring out their negative sides, resulting in an onslaught of attacks on the space's occupants. The best way to safeguard yourself and your valuables are with Metal to weaken its energy. According to Depletion Cycle theory, Metal can exhaust #5's Earth energy, helping repress its negative impact. You can be creative and come up with your own symbolic feng shui cures—just be sure to incorporate metal symbols and similar features. If avoiding #5 star is impossible, try these traditional feng shui cures: a metal wind chime with six rods, a brass pagoda, six ancient Chinese coins, a brass rooster, or brass celestial animals. The same metal sound method used in treating #2 star should apply here, as well. The #5 yellow star resides in the center sector in 2013. Its energy intensifies in the South, Southwest, and Northeast.

Star #6 (Metal)

The auspicious #6 white metal star represents unexpected investment and financial fortune. The Bagua denotes the sixth star as the "authority and power." If you need help from a mentor or from helpful and influential people during a difficult time, look to this lucky star. When #6 is paired with #8, it will show its majestic strength. Northeast and Southwest are two prime locations to set off its brilliance; however, when infected by #2's or #5's negative side, the result could be a dangerous condition leading to financial loss, disease, or illness. To enhance the positive feng shui and subdue the negative, use Metal. The #6 star resides in the Northwest in 2013.

Star #7 (Metal)

The dreadful #7 star is filled with hostility that causes instances of bloodletting, either physical or financial, to the occupants of a space. These might include injury, robbery, fraud, plagiarism, or forgery. Take notice of its whereabouts, especially when it joins with stars 2, 5, 6, and even with another 7—these pairings can be fatal in Northeast, Southwest, West, and Northwest. Use Metal when #7 blends with stars 2 or 5, and Water when it blends with #6 and #7 metal star. Apply Water cure when it joins with star 4, 7, or 9 to alleviate the effects of sexual misconduct or romantic scandals. The #7 star resides in the West in 2013.

Star #8 (Earth)

The most energetic star in the current Eighth Period is the #8 white star. It is charged with invigorating energy that showers its occupants with prosperity, good health, and cozy relationships. This most auspicious star, the main source of money luck, may be activated with Water in the

Southeast, and central sectors to ensure financial growth. Fortune will abound when it joins star 1, 6, 8, or 9 in the West, Northwest, Northeast, and South. Activate these pairings with Earth to promote good health and flourishing relationships with family and friends, especially in the Southwest and Northeast. The #8 star resides in the Northeast in 2013.

Star #9 (Fire)

The #9 purple star represents future financial luck, attracing helpful people to come to the aid of a career, growing business, or budding romance. It can also reinforce the energy of any stars with which it comes in contact, good or bad. Wealth and prosperity only get stronger when #9 is paired with star 1, 6, 8, or itself; however, it can become an incendiary star, bringing failure and fire hazards, if blended with star 2, 3, 5, or 7. So be on an alert when those stars infuse with #9 in the East, Southeast, Northeast, West, Southwest, and Northwest. Traditional feng shui cures employ Metal to overcome those negative energies. The #9 star resides in the South in 2013.

Beware of Malicious Stars

Every year there are five mischievous stars that make their way around our home or business, and we should take notice of and respect their existence in the sectors they inhabit for the year. The most harmful, #5 star, can be deadly, while the #2 star shows no mercy. Tai Sui Jupiter affects our emotions, while the Three Ruin Star can be aggravating. We should also be aware of the whereabouts of #3 and #7 stars, which have furious natures. Feng shui cures should be put in place, because you may not know when one of these stars will decide to strike.

Tai Sui General of Jupiter, a Tai Sui year of change, is currently underway for a few of the animal signs. Each year one of sixty Tai Sui Generals will rule the entire year and also directly impact four of the twelve animal signs. If you're one of the four affected with Tai Shui, it's important that you don't occupy or face its direction

Table-8d: Tai Shui Jupiter Yearly Location			
Year / Animal	Direction	Year / Animal	Direction
2011 Rabbit	East	2017 Rooster	West
2012 Dragon	Southeast	2018 Dog	Northwest
2013 Snake	Southeast	2019 Boar	Northwest
2014 Horse	South	2020 Rat	North
2015 Ram	Southwest	2021 Ox	Northeast
2016 Monkey	Southwest	2022 Tiger	Northeast

during the year. Tai Sui flies in the same order as the twelve animal signs each year.

Tai Sui resides in the Southeast in 2013, creating a tepid discord with Monkey and tiger, and seriously afflicting Boar, which is in the hot seat exactly opposite Tai Sui. The malicious star will reside in the South in 2014, which will affect Rat, Rooster, and Rabbit. When your animal sign is directly facing Tai Shui (the sixth spot from it in the twelve animal wheel), that year may be filled with mishaps and accidents for you. Here's what can happen: illnesses, relocation, legal problems (run-ins with authority), quarrels, injuries, flaring tempers and mood swings resulting from emotional distress, personal relationship issues, and involvement in ugly rumors and gossip. These are all characteristics of someone directly clashing with Tai Sui.

How bad things will be really depends on your karma, attitudes, and emotions. It's fair to ask yourself, *Have I been naughty or nice?* in order to predict what kind of situations may be headed your way. However, viewed from a positive perspective, Tai Sui is necessary for our spiritual growth. It forces us to be more aware of our thoughts, emotions, and conduct. Learning to handle and grow from our challenges is good for the soul.

If your animal sign falls under Tai Sui's ruling for the year, you shouldn't necessarily expect bad things to happen; you might just experience some dramatic changes in your life such as moving a residence or business, finding a new job, seeing changes in your education or finances, or perhaps a beginning a new relationship. Remember, the main theme here is change.

The best feng shui cures would be not sitting and facing or sleeping with your head pointed toward the Tai Sui direction. Keep that area quiet; do not break ground or start construction there so that you don't stir up unwanted energies in the area. If you must break ground, start on either adjacent side and then move toward the Tai Sui direction. For example, Tai Sui resides in Southeast for 2013; therefore, you could start groundbreaking either from the South or from the East and then proceed toward Southeast. Such a move would be considered safe.

Three Ruin Star is a dreadful star that brings bad luck in relationship, loss, betrayal, and fraud into your life. Each year it occupies the cardinal direction that corresponds with the three compatible animal signs. To avoid its attack, sit facing its direction and keep the afflicted area calm and quiet.

Table-8e Three-Ruin Star Yearly Location	
Cardinal Direction / Year	Animals Compatibility Year
South (2008, 2012, 2016)	Rat |Dragon | Monkey
East (2009, 2013, 2017)	Ox |Snake | Rooster
North (2010, 2014, 2018)	Tiger | Horse | Dog
West (2011, 2015, 2019)	Rabbit | Ram | Boar

Predicting Future Events

A lot of information can be gleaned from the Magic Square charts to help us predict future events. Here's what happened in 2011 and what was predicted for the couple of years that followed:

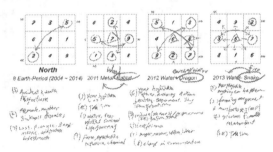

Diagram 8.5 *Flying Stars charts used for predicting future events.*

We can see that the year 2011 spelled trouble for Japan, as illustrated in the diagram. The tragic earthquake and tsunami that hit that country can be explained by the powerful and destructive combination of energies. Most notably, 2011 was a Metal year clashing with Wood Rabbit, associated with "shaking" circumstances. The meeting of annual #5 star and #6 Eighth Period star fueled the drama in the East, creating dangerous conditions with possible explosions and putting families in great danger. Furthermore, the Tai Sui star afflicted the East, as well, acting as a catalyst for and also fueling the destruction. Energies from opposite directions also had negative ramifications. Meanwhile, Northeast was affected by the conflicting energies of #1 annual star with #2 Eighth Period star.

The year 2012 was a combination of Water over Earth Dragon, which can be a telltale sign of natural disaster—although Dragon does contain some Water, which means there is plenty of water to support those in need of this element.

The highlight of 2012 was dramatic changes in the leadership in both the public and private sectors. In fact, we've already seen the effects of 2012 from the loss of Apple cofounder Steve Jobs in early October 2011, which marked the beginning of the trend, followed by the death of Libyan dictator Muammar Gadhafi and North Korea's Kim Jung-Il. We should be concerned about the year 2013, when heavenly Water clashes with earthly Snake's Fire. The combination suggests the possibility of natural disasters as well as wars, mine explosions, and devastating fires.

Here's why these events occurred: Diagram 8.5 shows a hostile #7 star, signifying loss, resided in the Northwest sector of the Magic Square, associated in Bagua with father, authority, or male. Meanwhile, #5 yellow star afflicted the Southeast, the wealth area of our home. Dragon is symbolically associated with transformation, connection, and freedom, and the year of the Dragon also emphasizes leadership, good and bad. Since #6 is a Metal star, representing money and gold, leadership in financial institutions generated big news. Many of the year's most notable events were related to finance—news about Wall Street, banking, currency, and gold that affected individuals and business. It wouldn't be a surprise to see men got into financial ruin. Some unfortunate souls may have lost their freedom or lives in 2012, though for others, 2012 may have been the year they become debt-free.

Most noticeable in the health area may be illnesses of the nervous and digestion systems and injuries to the lungs, mouth, limbs, or skin, especially to females and young children. On a positive note, many small businesses or individuals may have taken on new leadership roles in the year of transformation; it may have been a year of breaking through barriers and creating new projects and new adventures in some areas in the industry. It may also been a year of first spiritual awakenings for many people.

Other destructive energies came from Southeast and the gruesome misfortunes brought by star #5 and Tai Sui. In the Southwest there was a #3 star, which could have brought confrontations and battles, especially among female friends, in 2012. The deadliest storm ever to hit the northeastern part of the United States in late October was the result of #2 Eighth Period star magnified by the annual #9 and monthly #9 star. The devastating storm had taken many lives and caused serious damages resulting in big financial losses for many families.

Now, not all the news was bad: also in 2012, #6 star, representing heaven or the spirits, means celestial bodies was the focus. New astronomical discoveries had already surfaced, and there will be many more on the horizon. What's particularly interesting about 2012 was that many individuals have felt spiritually connected for the first time.

What troubles me is that we're still facing the possibility of a series of earthquakes, especially in the southwest, and they could be quite large and devastating. The threads of possibility will be higher as we get into last half of 2013 (Water Snake year), when Water and Fire will battle against one another and can create quite an explosive event—not just natural disasters, but possibly wars and massive explosions. Every star in 2013 is reverted back to its original position, so #5 is back in the center sector. That means all directions will be influenced by this star, with our health and relationships facing the greatest threat. On top of that, the 2013 chart indicates Eight Period #5 star is confronting yet another troubled star #2 in the Southwest relationship area affecting mothers and female friends. Earthquakes possibility is also at its highest while #3 brings confronting battle, legal matter, and bad rumor for the family.

Do your own analysis and try to predict future events using the Magic Square—see how close you get with your predictions. Refer to the Bagua, the twelve animal symbols, and the five elements tables to help you make your own life-event predictions for the coming years.

How to Construct a Feng Shui Map of Your Building

The Effects of Combining Stars

There are many different star combinations, each of which will produce a different series of conditions leading to certain events and situations. So all combinations must be considered when it comes to feng shui analysis and prediction. Sometimes bad combinations can have serious negative consequences, bringing hostility that makes an entire area of a structure temporarily unusable. In that case it would be wise to get out of the way altogether. Generally speaking, it's always a good idea to go with the flow, adapting to changing conditions in order to reduce life's many struggles. For example, to protect your health, sleep in an area of the house that will not bring you harm. Consider buying an air mattress or sleeping bag; it's worth the investment.

So how do you know what area of the house is good for you? In order to see these invisible energies, you'll need a map indicating where the energy current flows in your building.

Determine the Quality of Chi in Your Building

This is a popular method commonly practiced by feng shui enthusiasts because it involves up-close observations of a space over time. A building can be affected by one of many energy fields depending on its orientation. There are two ways to approach the construction of a Flying Star chart. One is to use the Bagua method, which can help if you do not know when the building was constructed. The other, more complex method is based solely on the building's construction year; either the construction year or the "renewed" year (when the building was renovated) is used to determine a building's energy field and strength.

Flying Stars: Method One
Use this method if you do not know when your structure was built and if it has not had any extensive renovations in the past twenty years.

1. To construct the chart, determine a Bagua building type based on its sitting direction (opposite the facing direction). For example, a North-sitting building will have #1 in the center grid; a South-sitting will have #9 in the center. You may select one of eight possible facing directions, as shown in diagram 8.6.
2. Fill in the yearly stars beginning at the lower right of the main number.
3. Make twelve complete yearly charts, and then fill in the monthly Flying Star numbers, beginning at the lower left, next to each of the main star numbers. Once that's complete you will have an entire year's view of where chi has settled temporarily within your building. Use this information to help you make analyses in your investigation.
4. When studying the charts, analyze the potential impact of pairings between a main star and an annual star or an annual star and a monthly star. Pay attention to any other influences in the same sector or direction that may trigger an event or series of events. Display appropriate feng shui symbols in those areas, paying attention to which symbolic materials might cause disharmony within a sector. Refer to chapter 9 for a list of symbols that may work for you.

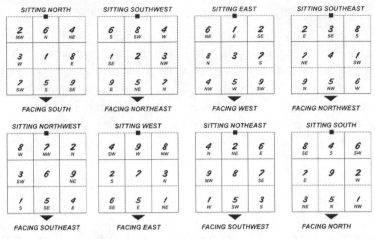

Diagram 8.6 *The eight Bagua building types.*

Flying Stars: Method Two

Before we move on to the next method, double-check your building's construction year. The Magic Square map of sitting and facing stars can be generated only from this piece of information.

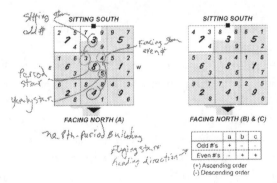

Diagram 8.7 *A Flying Stars chart of an Eighth Period building. The map reveals in detail the quality of energy in the space within a twenty-year span.*

There are three key factors in this method: the building period (construction year); the sitting stars (a.k.a. mountain stars), which are associated with Earth elements that affect our health and relationships; and the facing stars (a.k.a. water stars), which are associated with Water elements and have a strong influence on our material wealth—areas like our personal possessions and careers.

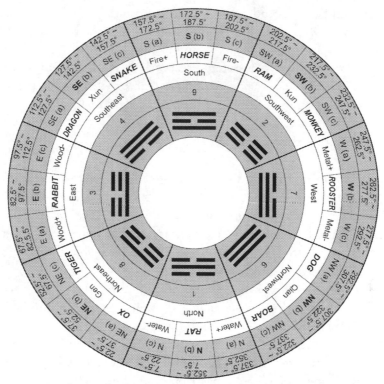

Diagram 8.8 *The twenty-four subdivisions of eight directions are used to identify the exact "sitting" or "facing" orientation of a building.*

Here is how you construct your map:

Let's assume you know your building's construction year. Refer to table 8b to determine your building's period number and place it in the center grid; then complete the entire chart. Next you will need to fill in the rest of the numbers of sitting stars, which are directly opposite the facing stars. Begin by using a compass to measure the angle of your building's facing side to ascertain its direction. Then refer to diagram 8.8, the twenty-four subdivision wheel, to determine which of the three subdivisions (a, b, or c) is your building's true facing direction. For example, a 340-degree angle will put the facing due North (a), while a 5-degree angle places it due North (b) and a 20-degree angle would be due North (c).

The next step is to fill in the whole chart with numbers, as illustrated in diagram 8.7, above. Fill in the first sitting star number (left) and the first facing star number (right) in the center grid, where Period 8 star has established the foundation of the map. Then determine whether these numbers will fly in ascending or descending order. There are two factors involved in the flying pattern: (1) the orientation of the building; and (2) the odd or even number of the sitting/facing stars in the center sector, which will determine the heading direction. There's an exception to this rule: if either star's number is 5, the oddness or evenness of the active period will be used to determine its heading direction.

Do this if you know either your building's construction year or its "renewed" (renovation) year:

1. Determine the building period—refer to table 8b to obtain the main number to be placed in the center grid. Complete the chart with all nine stars.
2. Fill in the sitting and facing stars on your chart, or select the one from diagrams 8.9–8.13 that fits your building's orientation and building period.
3. Fill in the current yearly stars (smaller number) pattern; place numbers to the lower right of each main star (bigger number). Refer to diagram 8.7 for an illustration.
4. When studying the charts, analyze the potential impact between a main star and the annual and monthly stars in the same sector; the impacts of sitting and facing stars have the greatest influence in the space, so they deserve the most attention. Take note of any other influences in the same sector that might act as the catalyst for a possible event or series of events. Display appropriate feng shui symbols in the area, paying attention to the materials you use and whether they will create harmony or bring conflict to the sector. Refer to chapter 9 for a list of symbols that may work for you.

The Magic Formulas for Reaching Common Dreams

Looking for a magic formula to improve certain areas of your life? Well, there is such a thing. Follow the feng shui formulas below for your home and office in order to attract good fortune. As you may already know, the outcome may be limited or influenced by many factors, including your own skills, commitment, trust, patience, and health.

When incorporating feng shui into a building's design, arrange key architectural features like its layout, rooms, landscape, and pool with your long-term purpose in mind. These features should correspond to the Bagua symbolic meanings and their directions. Non-fixed features should be adaptable to the ever-changing yearly energies in accordance with Flying Stars principles. When determining feng shui cures or enhancements, remember to apply the theory of the five elements and their natural cycles as well as symbols, sculptures, figures, images, shapes, colors, aromas, and sounds. The size of the objects should not be too large or too small, and they do not have to be traditional Chinese feng shui objects, as long they have special meaning to you. They are simply physical objects of affirmation that reflect our emotions and communicate with our subconscious mind. Being mentally aware of the process will make our feng shui even more powerful. The energy of the symbols used should resonate strongly with us since their subtle energies influence us deeply, at the subconscious level. That said, some traditional cures—such as the dragon, crane, turtle, goldfish, three-legged toad, and pagoda, as well as bamboo and celestial animals—have earned the approval of feng shui communities all over the world because they've worked remarkably well for many people.

1. To Promote Good Physical and Mental Health

Protect your health from harmful forces while enhancing your luck.
You'll need a healthy mind and body to enjoy the happy life you're striving so hard to attain. For this reason alone it is worth your effort to set up feng shui every year. You'll want to implement techniques that both support and strengthen your life energy. Work to promote healthy balance on the seven chakra points; refer to diagram 5.1 for details.

1. Meditate regularly for five to thirty minutes or more, saying a prayer to end each session; prayer provides hope and serves as affirmation. Implement chi-kung or tai chi to encourage chi circulation, as well as to remove and renew harmful, stagnant chi.
2. Express your feelings in drawing or writing, and then burn the paper. That's a powerful symbol of letting go of your trapped emotions so new feelings can emerge.
3. Eat foods that can provide a boost to your life element.
4. Implement Metal cures to any sectors of the building that contain #2 star or #5 star on the charts, especially when both stars are in the same sector. Pay attention to the monthly star, which may be the trigger for an implosion. Think creatively:

beside wind chimes, the sound of a piano, a music box, or bells can hold down these stars' harmful effects. Shy away from Earth element in these sectors.

5. If you are recovering from an illness, it would be best to stay out of the inflicted areas for the time being and keep the windows closed, especially when combined with stars 2, 3, 5, or 7. The impact can be deadly. Locate and strengthen #8 star with Earth to boost your health. Display symbols or statues of deities, angels, turtles, cranes, lotus flowers, or peaches, all associated with longevity.

6. Support East with Green color and Wood—ideally something that does not conflict with visiting stars. Place bamboo or herb plants and lotus flowers in the East. Bamboo is a symbol for growth and expansion. Herbs have healing properties, while lotus has many symbolic meanings, including longevity. A moon or a phoenix symbolizes renewal.

7. Determine your kua number. See table 7d to find your four favorable directions. Sit facing your sheng-qi (first) direction; sleep with your head pointing toward your tian yi (second) or fu wei (fourth) direction. If possible, avoid your four unfavorable directions.

8. Beware of any negative impact if your animal sign is currently in conflict with Tai Sui. If you are clashing with Tai Sui, follow some of the remedies suggested earlier. Also take care of yourself: watch your diet; exercise regularly; postpone any big plans or projects, and get plenty of sleep. Wear or place emerald or jade stones to stimulate good health. Clear quartz crystals and amethysts bring excellent healing properties to a space.

9. Remove any object(s) with sharp edges or corners pointing toward your bed, because they create killing chi, which can be harmful to your health. If this object cannot be removed, such as a roof, a column, or built-in bookshelves, place furniture, trees, or plants in between you and it to block its effects. A convex mirror can do the job, although a traditional Bagua mirror cannot be placed inside the house, as it can attract unwanted spirits. Avoid sleeping under an exposed beam, as it can suppress your chi and bring troublesome symptoms to any part of your body that is directly under it.

2. To Attract Love and Relationships

Attract someone into your life by stimulating the chemistry in yourself and those in contact with you.

If the current year is compatible with your sign, it favors your love and relationship areas, which of course increases your chances of meeting a mate. Besides indicating your possible compatibility, the Liu-he animal month and/or year are a perfect time to seize any opportunity that comes your way.

1. Invigorate your mood for finding new love by placing written affirmation under your pillow. Do five to thirty minutes of relaxation meditation regularly, followed by verbal affirmation of your desires. Place your trust in the universe and yourself, taking action from the cues given by your intuition to meet other people.
2. Express your feelings by drawing or writing them on paper, and then burn it. That's a powerful symbol of letting go of your trapped emotions so new feelings can emerge.
3. Take advantage of the liu-he animal signs for the month or the year to help you meet a potential mate.
4. Determine your kua number. See table 7d for your four favorable directions. Sit facing your sheng-qi (first) direction; sleep with your head pointing toward your yan nian (third) direction.
5. Create a warm and cozy atmosphere in your bedroom. Display in the Southwest pictures of your sweetheart and symbols or images of love suggesting union and passionate affection, such as a couple in a romantic setting, a pair of swallows or mandarin ducks, or a dragon and a phoenix. Brighten this sector or room with a pair of red candles in the Southwest corner, creating pleasant views and aromas there. The colors and materials of your bed and bedding play a role in setting your emotional state, as well, so be selective in your choices. Display and/or wear rose quartz crystal jewelry to spur on romantic moments. These efforts can have a great impact on your subconscious, so put your energy into them.
6. To enhance your social and relationships, look for any combination of the lucky romance stars #1 and #4 in a sector.

Then strengthen their energies with yin Water and Wood element (like a water bamboo plant). You can do more to enhance the setting by energizing the sector with pleasant colors, views, and aromas.

7. Locate and enhance #8 star with crystals, ideally rose quartz. It will help spark your chance for a new relationship and keep it stable.

8. Suppress #3, the quarrel star, because it might sabotage your plan; use Fire element to keep it under control, wherever it may be residing.

9. Locate Tai Sui and Three Ruin star in any of the sectors and apply remedies as needed.

3. Eliminate Quarrels and Bitter Fights and Prevent Run-Ins with the Law

The ramifications of these stars can make someone turn bitter for no apparent reason. Too often we see people clash with one another, kicking off a long, miserable battle. That's because when their energy levels vibrate at the same frequency, they attract each other and collide—sometimes literally, as with car accidents.

1. Stay calm and in control of your emotions when dealing with others, especially with friends whose zodiac signs are incompatible with yours. Reconciling yourself to difficult circumstances can ease your frustration or even remove your inner struggles. Remember to view the situation from various perspectives, and when appropriate, be willing to accept, adapt, and change. By doing so, you will have contained your ego and not allowed it to control you.

2. Express your frustration in two ways: (1) physically release your built-up tension by exercising or playing sports; and (2) express your feelings by drawing or writing on paper and then burning it. That's a powerful symbol of letting go of your trapped emotions so new feelings can emerge.

3. Meditate regularly for five to thirty minutes or more, working on your peace and serenity to subdue your anger and frustration. Say a prayer to end each session; prayer provides hope and serves as affirmation, as well.

4. Wear an amulet made of clear quartz crystal or amethyst; jade will work wonderfully too. See table 5a for other ways to use stones.

5. Give the building or room a proper cleansing ritual to clear out negative energy. Open doors and windows, burn incense and candles, and play the sound of a bell. After the ceremony, lift the room's spirits with fragrant aromas.

6. Display images or symbols of a god, goddess, or angel to remind us of kind and gentle feelings (e.g., the Laughing Buddha).

7. Locate #3 star on the chart, as it could become a furious star in the East and Southeast, Wood territories. Subdue its adverse effects with Fire—the colors red and pink are preferable to using physical fire. Remove any Wood (all plants) in the area. If possible, avoid any area where #3 star is combined with stars 2, 3, 5, or 7.

8. Locate Tai Sui and Three Ruin stars in the sector, and avoid sleeping in the area if possible. Beware of the possible negative impact if your animal sign is currently in conflict with Tai Sui. If you are clashing with Tai Sui, apply the suggested remedies.

9. Locate #8 star on the chart and strengthen your relationship area by placing Earth in that sector. A symbol of harmony, such as a large ceramic vase that depicts images of happiness, would be perfect.

4. Encourage Prosperity and Preserve Wealth
Locate and enhance wealth stars in your home or office for abundant growth.

1. Meditate regularly for five to thirty minutes or more; say a prayer to end each session. Prayer provides hope and serves as affirmation, as well. Implement any kind of exercise program to release any subconscious buildup of tension. A healthy mind and body will produce clear and creative thinking and emit positive energy with potential to attract money and business opportunities. Express your feelings by drawing or writing them on paper, and then burn it. That's a powerful symbol

of letting go of your trapped emotions so new feelings can emerge.

2. Eat the foods that will provide a boost to your life element.

3. Activate the Southeast "wealth" sector with Wood reinforced with Water. Place books and magazines about personal, business, and investment growth in this area.

4. Locate the yearly #8 major wealth stars on the chart, and then reinforce those sectors with Earth elements such as boulders, precious stones, and quartz crystals. Fire can also be used for enhancement. In Method Two, if #8 is a water star (facing star), activate its energy with Water.

5. To preserve your resources and prevent future losses, locate #7 star and exhaust its negative effects with still Water, such as a large vase filled with water. Locate Tai Sui and Three Ruin stars and apply remedies in those sectors as needed.

6. Apply the San-he method (optional): display your compatible animal figurines in auspicious directions.

7. Apply the Eight House method, referring to table 7d to find the two wealth positions in your building. Activate the energy in the sector that corresponds to the Bagua symbol. This may conflict with the element of the visiting (annual or monthly) stars, so you will have to make an intuitive decision. Promote money luck for individual family members: determine the kua number from table 7c in order to obtain your four favorable directions. Then sit facing or sleep with your head pointing toward your sheng-qi (first) direction. The yan nian (third) direction is your second wealth position.

8. Place large boulders to represent mountains in the Northeast and a water pond (pool) in the Southwest for the duration of the Eighth Period (2003–2014). This setup can be designed to work both indoors and outdoors. The water must be clean and healthy, as dirty water will create stagnant chi that stops growth while breeding diseases.

9. Display a pair of celestial animals like fu dog (qilin) at the front door for wealth protection; choose the material for the sector accordingly whenever possible. Place a money vault made of metal in the Northwest for males and Southwest for females, and keep valuable assets like jewelry, gold, and silver coins inside the vault to suggest prosperity and security. Wealth

symbols can spark auspicious energy, so they are absolutely appropriate to use.

This step may be skipped or, when appropriate, applied together with the Flying Stars method. According to the Form School method, the area diagonally across from the door-swing at the entrance of a room is the "wealth" location. Place an aquarium there filled with nine goldfish, one of them black. Goldfish symbolize abundance and prosperity; eight is the most auspicious number for wealth, while nine represents long-lasting fortune.

5. Career Opportunities, Academic Achievements, and Growth

Attract career opportunities and helpful people to give you a boost in your career. Picking up new skills or doing well in school are always great ways to ensure career growth.

1. Do five to thirty minutes of meditation regularly, as it can help produce clear, creative thinking; this helps the brain process activities better while refreshing the mind so it absorbs information more easily. Say a prayer to end each session; prayer provides hope and serves as affirmation. Implement any kind of exercise program to release the subconscious buildup of tension. A healthy mind and body will result in positive thinking and clearer thoughts, which will help you achieve your goals. Express your feelings by drawing or writing them on paper, and then burn it. That's a powerful symbol of letting go of your trapped emotions so new feelings can emerge.
2. Eat the foods that can provide a boost to your life element.
3. Locate your work desk in the Northeast ("wisdom and knowledge") sector, and sit facing your sheng-qi (first) direction or yan nian (third) direction. Display blue or green candles in the sector to suggest academic and self-development successes.
4. Set up the career area in the North sector with a Water element: hang up a picture of a waterfall, images representing your dream careers, and written affirmations of your desires.
5. Stimulate #6 star with Metal and Earth; this star invites supporters, mentors, and helpful people into your life,

which may lead to many opportunities for the future. For a business, locate the marketing and public relations staff in the Northwest.

6. Place books and magazines related to business and investment growth in the Southeast.
7. Activate the auspicious #8 star in its sector to strengthen your relationships with others and set the proper conditions for welcoming financial growth.
8. The #4 star can help you accomplish your academic goals: locate and enhance it with Wood and Water. If it combines with #1 white star, that's even better.
9. Locate Tai Sui and Three Ruin stars and apply remedies to those sectors as needed.

6. Fame and Popularity
Bring fame and popularity into your life and business. Become a prominent figure with influence on society.

1. Meditate regularly for five to thirty minutes or more, saying a prayer to end each session. Prayer provides hope and serves as affirmation. Implement any kind of exercise program to release the subconscious buildup of tension. A healthy mind and body will produce clear and creative thinking and emit positive energy into the universe, attracting opportunities and events to make you popular.
2. Do a few sessions of self-hypnosis to remove past negative feelings that may be blocking good energy. This technique can make you feel renewed and help you free yourself from any resistance deep inside.
3. Express your feelings by drawing or writing them on paper, and then burn it. That's a powerful symbol of letting go of your trapped emotions so new feelings can emerge.
4. Fire is the main element for the explosive energy of fame. Make use of Wood in your setup in the South, but you'd be better off not to enhance Fire when stars 2 and 5 reside there.
5. Locate #9 star and strengthen it with Wood.
6. Store books and magazines related to fame and fortune in the South. Display awards, diplomas, and other symbols of recognition.

7. Stop bad rumors by locating the trouble-making #3 star and weakening it with Fire or, alternately, the color red or pink.

8. Locate Tai Sui and Three Ruin stars and apply remedies to those sectors as needed.

9. Locate #8 star on the chart and strengthen its influence on your social relationships by using Earth and Fire in that sector. The phoenix symbol depicts illumination in your life.

7. Fertility
This remedy will create the ideal conditions—spiritually, that is—for conception.

1. Do a few sessions of self-hypnosis to remove past negative feelings and old beliefs that may be preventing you from getting pregnant. This technique can make you feel renewed while helping you free yourself from any resistance deep inside. Express your feelings by drawing or writing them on paper, and then burn it. A symbol of letting go of your trapped emotions so new feelings can emerge. You can also invigorate your mood for love by placing written affirmation under a pillow. Consider hanging charms on the wall; they can be powerful emotional triggers. Implement chi-kung or tai chi to encourage chi circulation; the regular practice of chi-kung is said to have a good success rate in treating infertility, and it removes and renews harmful, stagnant chi.

2. Do five to thirty minutes of relaxation and meditation regularly, paying close attention to your sacral chakra. Follow it with verbal affirmation of your desires, and end each session with a prayer, which provides hope and acts as affirmation. Table 5a may help shed some light into your concern.

3. Determine your kua number, using table 7d to find your favorable directions. Sit facing and sleep with your head pointing toward your sheng-qi (first) direction. If possible, avoid your unfavorable directions entirely.

4. If possible, activate the East sector of the home and bedroom with Water and Wood. Place books about and display images of happy babies and small children playing in a garden or on a playground. Display an image of your god or goddess associated with granting offspring, like Guan Yin holding

a baby. Among other images known for promoting fertility: children with mother, a garden, the moon, a lake, fruit trees, a pomegranate, a pearl, a spiral, and emeralds.

5. Create a warm and cozy atmosphere in your bedroom. Display in the Southwest a picture of your sweetheart and a symbol or image that would suggest union and passionate affection, like a couple in a romantic candlelit setting or a pair of mandarin ducks. Brighten this sector or room with pleasant views and aromas. The color and materials of your bed and bedding can affect your emotional state, as well, so be selective in your choices. Display and/or wear rose crystal jewelry to inspire romance. These efforts can have a great impact on your subconscious, so put your energy into them.

6. Locate and enhance #8 star with the Earth element crystal—ideally rose quartz. This will help spark an intimate relationship with your partner and keep it stable.

7. Implement Metal cures to any sector of the building that contains stars 2 or 5, especially if it contains both stars. Get creative: besides wind chimes, the sound of a piano, a music box, or even bells could reduce the stars' harmful effects. Shy away from using Earth elements in this sector, and keep the windows and doors closed whenever possible for the entire year.

8. Locate the Tai Sui and Three Ruin stars and apply remedies to those sectors as needed. It's best not to occupy those rooms.

9. Suppress the #3 annual star, which might create tension between you and your partner: use Fire to keep its energy under control wherever it may be residing.

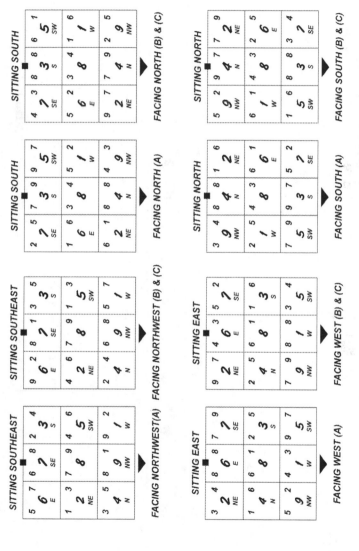

Diagram-8.9a 8th Period (2004 ~2023) East-Group Building

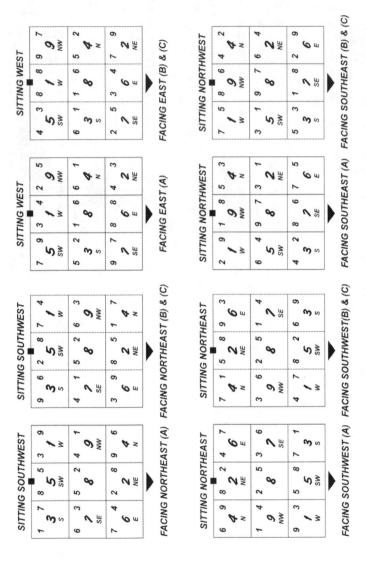

Diagram-8.9b 8th Period (2004 ~ 2023) West-Group Building

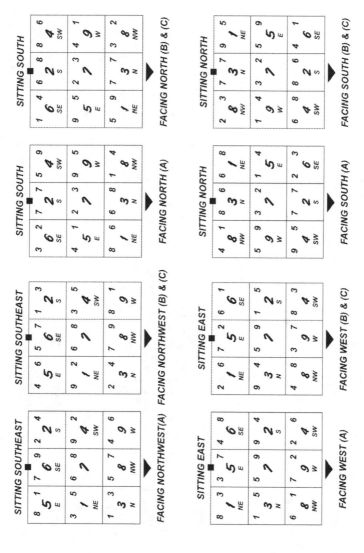

Diagram-8.10a 7th Period (1984~2003) East-Group Building

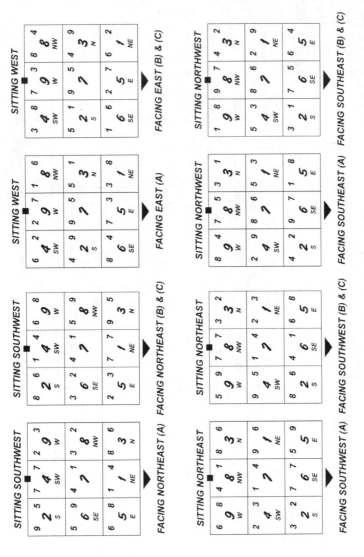

Diagram-8.10b 7th Period (1984 ~ 2003) West-Group Building

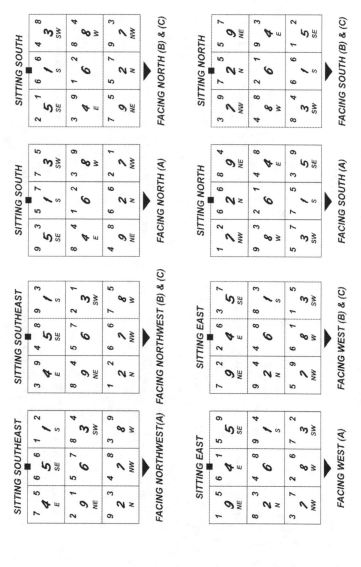

Diagram-8.11a 6th Period (1964 ~1983) East-Group Building

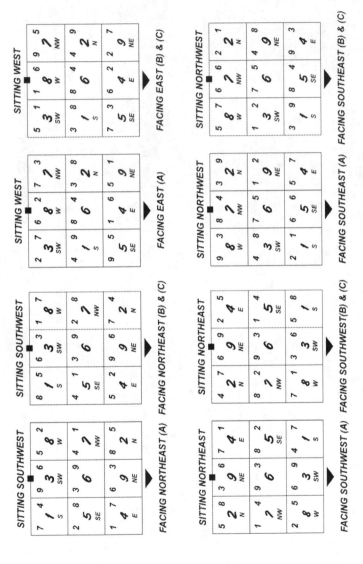

Diagram-8.11b 6th Period (1964 ~ 1983) West-Group Building

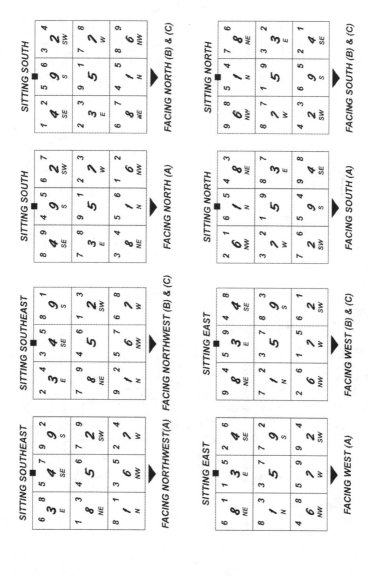

Diagram-8.12a 5th Period (1944 ~1963) East-Group Building

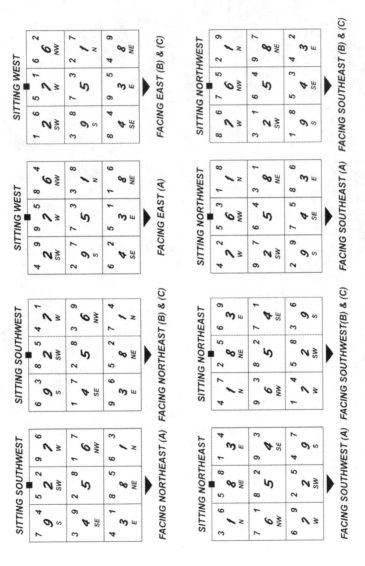

Diagram-8.12b 5th Period (1944 ~ 1963) West-Group Building

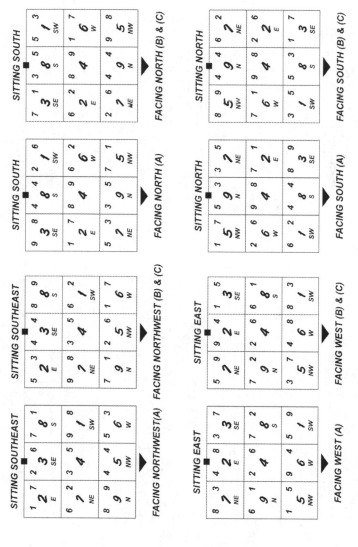

Diagram-8.13a 4th Period (1924 ~1943) East-Group Building

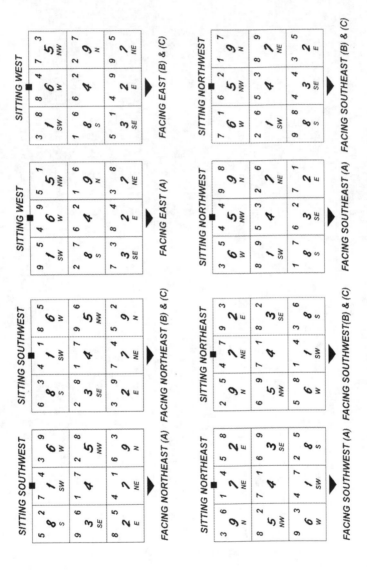

Diagram-8.13b 4th Period (1924 ~ 1943) West-Group Building

Chapter 9

Quick Feng Shui Tips and Symbolism

Beds

The bed is where your body rests and revitalizes your chi, so you must give it some careful thought. Here are a few suggestions.

- It's best to sleep in a bedframe made of materials that align with your kua elements.
- Sleep with your head pointing toward your most favorable directions.
- Position your headboard against a wall for support.
- Do not hang a painting or other artwork depicting water above your headboard, as it denotes drowning.

Chi Flow

Certain types of energy (chi) tend to flow in certain areas. There are several factors that influence this difference, most notably the size of the space and the objects within it.

- Sheng-qi, or vital chi, flows in big, open spaces.
- Sha-qi, or killing chi, is caused by straight roads, sharp corners, or pointed objects.
- Si-qi, or dead chi, is stagnant, dead energy, found in cluttered space, in an abandoned room or dirty pond, and in withered plant, as well.

Cluttered Spaces

The first thing you should do to create good feng shui is remove clutter in the building. This will remove stagnant or dead chi in the space and encourage the free flow of energy, thereby removing obstacles in your life.

Colors

Select the colors of your house, automobile, and personal accessories to match your life kua element: green for Wood; red/pink for Fire; yellow/brown for Earth; metallic/white for Metal; and blue/black for Water.

Exception: black is generally not recommended as a ceiling or wall color, as it can suggest sadness or the dark side of life.

Wealth Fortune

If you want good luck, you must get in tune with the powerful energy flows of the universe. For twenty years of good luck in the areas of health, relationships, and wealth, place Earth (like a mountain symbol) in Northeast and Water (a water feature) in the Southwest sector of the property. Make sure the water flows toward the building and not away from it.

Crystals

Precious stones are ideal for activating the Earth element. They are also used as tools for all kinds of health benefits.

Elements Natural Cycles

Wood, Fire, Earth, Metal, and Water, the five universal elements in the universe, are the basis of the feng shui system. Each element exists in interrelationship with the others, as indicated in the four elemental cycles:

- Generative Cycle
- Depletion Cycle
- Destructive Cycle
- Moderating Cycle

Exposed Ceiling Beams

An exposed ceiling beam presents a health hazard to anyone sleeping directly under it.

Figurines

For hundreds of thousands of years, these popular figurines have been used to attract good luck or repel bad luck:

- Money toads attract wealth.
- Turtles promote healing, longevity, and stability.
- Happy Buddha brings happiness and good fortune.
- Kwan-Kung General chases away evil spirits.
- A pair of celestial animals such as qilin, fu dogs, and lions by the front entrance provide protection and attract good luck.

Furniture

The material of furniture (e.g., bedframe, desk, and chair) in a certain sector should correspond to the element in that sector according to the Bagua or Magic Square layout.

Front Doors

The front entrance is highly important to the well-being of a building's occupants, since chi enters and exits there. Locate your front door in an auspicious area whenever possible. Doors must be both appealing and sturdy—after all, they are the gates to the castle.

Geometric Shapes

Shapes are symbols of the energy of the five elements, and like other such symbols, they can be applied in feng shui cures. Remember that the key to creating good feng shui is balance and symmetry.

- Rectangle: Wood
- Triangle: Fire
- Square: Earth
- Circle: Metal
- Curve: Water

Sha-qi (Killing Chi)

Look around for sharp edges or pointed corners on objects in your surrounding area. These create potentially harmful energies directed toward you or your building, so if possible, remove them or cover them up. Trees and plants can be used as barriers to block such negative energies. It's also acceptable to place something pleasant in between you and the projecting object(s).

Pets

Pets release energies too, so they can be implemented in feng shui. Know where to place your pets' bed or habitat once you've determined where their energies will help the most.

- Wood: cat and rabbit
- Fire: horse
- Earth: dog, bird, turtle
- Metal: frog
- Water: fish

Landscape: Black Tortoise, Green Asian Dragon, White Tiger, and Red Phoenix

This setup, which originated in the Form School, was one of the most prominent systems in the early history of feng shui, and it is still considered very auspicious and powerful. It was used by kings and nobles to sustain their empires, and later by farmers to locate fertile soil for their fields. Here is the setup:

The high mountains, Black Tortoise, lay in the back of a village, acting as support. To the front of the Tortoise there were lower hills on the right side representing the Green Asian Dragon, and the lowest hills on the left side representing the White Tiger, protecting the village from natural storms. A river for transporting goods spanned the land from left to right. A small hill, a symbol of the Red Phoenix, was at the front gate of the village, completing the setup. Today this ancient method is usually created artificially in the landscape with the symbolic use of large boulders, walls, trees and shrubs, fountains, and ponds.

Lighting

Lighting is a Fire element that can be used to subdue the destructive energy #3 star. Lighting is also used extensively in feng shui to direct and attract chi, e.g., to "lift" a low ceiling or the area below a staircase, or to fill in the negative space in an odd-shaped building.

Low Ceilings

A low ceiling can suppress your life chi, creating uneasiness or disturbing behavior. A high ceiling space accumulates vital chi, which is good for health and wealth.

Mirrors

Mirrors are awesome for bringing outdoor views into a house or visually expanding a narrow space. A concave mirror draws in energy, while a convex mirror deflects energy away. Place convex mirrors near your windows and doors to deflect away killing chi.

Numbers

While numbers may have different meanings in your culture, feng shui associates certain numbers with either positive or negative life-force energy.

Auspicious numbers: 1, 4, 6, 8, 9
Inauspicious numbers: 2, 3, 5, 7

Paths

Paths leading to the entrance of a home or building should be curvy, because straight roads generate killing chi while encouraging energy to rush past too quickly. A good feng shui path is meandering in order to generate vital chi—and even more so when it is accompanied by pleasant views and the fragrant scent of flowers. A path that narrows at the entrance directs energy into the building and is regarded as auspicious. A T-junction path generates sha-chi, killing energy that can jeopardize your health. Trees and tall shrubs used as barriers make a great cure.

Rooms

The space where you spend most of your time deserves thorough analysis and careful planning. Your bedroom is where your body renews itself, so make sure you feel good there. Clean it regularly to remove stagnant energy—a new moon is an ideal time for purifying the room. A ringing bell, scented candles, and burning incense are generally used in a ritual for cleansing.

- If a quarrel or unhappy event occurs in a room, open the doors and windows to let negative energy dissipate to the outside and to bring in fresh air.
- Too much water in the bedroom can bring you bad luck, financial loss, and scandals. Therefore, an aquarium in the bedroom is not recommended.
- Too many plants in the bedroom can disrupt your sleep. Sharp, pointed plants are not recommended indoors.
- Avoid sleeping or sitting under an overhead beam, as it can suppress your growth.
- Do not sleep with your feet pointing to the door—that symbolizes death. (A corpse is carried out of a room feet-first.)
- Avoid displaying pictures or objects that are depressing or gruesome.
- Introduce into your décor warm, pleasant colors that work well with your life kua element.

Stairs

Stairs behave like wind currents, carrying energy from one place to another.

- A staircase carries energies such as wealth, so it should not descend toward your front door (unless you want your fortune to rush out of the house).
- Avoid locating your front doors under a staircase, which will suppress your growth.
- The edges of steps can create harmful energies directed toward you or your house, affecting your health.

Symmetry

Feng shui is all about balance. All aspects of a space must be considered in order to create a harmonious environment that suits our body and spirit. Give some thought to shape, color, material, texture, lighting, sound, and aroma.

Trees

Consider planting trees such as bamboo and money trees in the Southeast or East for encouraging wealth, good health, and harmony in the family. Most fruit trees are symbols of abundance and fertility. Avoid planting mulberry trees because their name sounds like the Chinese word for "sorrow." Lilac, cactus, and wild rose are inauspicious because their prickly and thorny nature can create disharmony.

Water

Water energy is free-flowing and always ends at the lowest point; therefore it is thought to accumulate chi. Moving water is yang, while still water is yin; either can be used to activate the Water element in a particular sector. A pond or aquarium with nine fish represents long-lasting financial luck.

Symbolism, Signs, and Emblems

Signs are a powerful way to relate information, while symbols can convey simple ideas into larger and even more powerful meanings. Some symbols are universal, while others can have entirely different meanings in different cultures. Every culture has symbols and emblems that are associated with religious or spiritual beliefs, and they can be used for feng shui purposes. More elaborate meanings for some of the symbols and representations below can be found in *1001 Symbols* by Jack Tresidder, *Chinese Symbolism and Art Motifs* by C. A. S. Williams, and *The Handbook of Tibetan Buddhist Symbols* by Robert Beer. Build on this list by adding symbols and their meanings from your own culture.

Symbols

Animal: intuitive and physical power

Ash: death and rebirth

Bagua (Eight Trigrams): the cycles and evolution of nature

Bat (Five Bats): the five blessings in Chinese culture (longevity, wealth, health, virtue, and natural death); "evil" in Western culture

Bamboo: growth, expansion, flexibility, longevity

Bear: strength, bravery

Bee: community, sociability, diligence, creativity, frugality, industriousness, administration

Begging Bowl (a.k.a. Sacred Bowl, alms bowl): dharma, Buddhist teaching, humility, thoughts resonating into the universe

Bell: divine voice, protection against/dispersion of evil spirits

Bodhi Tree: wisdom, meditation

Bone: death

Broom: sweeping away obstacles, warding off evil spirits

Buddha: the "Enlightened One" a.k.a. Shakyamuni Buddha, founder of Buddhism, and a symbol of great wisdom, benevolence, unconditional love, and compassion

Celestial Animal: the four mythical creatures (dragon, phoenix, tortoise, and quilin)

Circle: wholeness, infinity, shield of protection, divine power, sun, eternity, peace, harmony, dignity, authority, and the origin of all creation

Cicada: immortality, resurrection, longevity

Candles: celebration of life, new beginning, fame, reputation

Coins (Ancient Chinese): prosperity. (When tied with string, they attract good luck or ward off evil spirits.)

Colors: life-force energy of the five elements—red, yellow, white, blue, and green. (Red is an auspicious color that brings happiness and wards off evil spirits; black is associated with yin, darkness, sorrow, evil, and death.)

Crow: auspicious in Asian culture but symbolizes war, death, and bad omens in Western culture

Dog: loyalty, guardian, protection

Door Gods: left and right doors as guardians warding off evil spirits

Dragon (Asian): the fifth orders of terrestrial branches, strength, transformation, wisdom, spirituality, vigilance, protection

Dream: communication from the subconscious or spirits

Earth: grounded and centered, health

Eclipse: inauspicious, signaling the loss of integrity of a ruler or leader

Eye: vigilance, protection, divinity

Fire: one of five elements, yang energy, sun, pure spirit, rising spirit, illumination, enlightenment, emotions, destruction, energy of change (creation and destruction)

Fish: prosperity, abundance

Five Elements: Wood, Fire, Earth, Metal, Water—the five forces or sources of creation emanating from the yin-yang principle

Flowers: sensual love, beauty, joy

Forest: subconscious, intuition

Frog: money-making opportunity, fertility, rain, water

Goddess of Mercy: Bodhisattva (Pusa) Guan Yin, worshipped for her protection and guidance, for bringing hope, and for her powers to cure infertility

God of Happiness, Longevity, and Wealth: auspicious three treasures

Goddess of the Sea (Queen of Heaven, Ma-Zu): safe journey

God of War: protection, justice, literacy, wealth

God of Wealth: prosperity and wealth

God of Wisdom: Bodhisattva Manjusri, a symbol of good omens, virtue, and bravery, and a great teacher

Gold: divinity

Goldfish: wealth, prosperity, good luck

Gourd: good health, longevity

Hand: protection, power, healing, union

Harmony: lute, sweet rice cake, mandala, circle, music, garden, vase

Head: chi, power, strength, authority

Heart: spirit, mind, love, compassion, courage, truth

Horse: speed, perseverance, success, victory

I Ching (the "Book of Changes," written by Fu Yi): one of the great treasures of China, used mainly for divination and thought to ward off evil spirits; the origin of feng shui

Koi fish: courage, endurance

Laughing Buddha: Maitreya Buddha, symbol of righteousness, kindness, and happiness

Lily: purity, virginity

Lotus: enlightenment, spiritual wisdom, purity, nirvana, fertility, rebirth, creation, sun, Buddhist Wheel of The Law

Lute: harmony, friendships, happiness, resonance, strength

Mandarin Duck and Wild Goose: fidelity, faithfulness

Mirror: hanging outside a building, wards off evil spirits or deflects negative influences from the environment

Numbers: fortune, life-force energy. (Numbers 6 and 8 are lucky, 5 and 13 are unlucky, and 3 is a charm and decision maker associated with success.)

Ocean or Sea: subconscious, power, strength, mystery, possibility

Octagon: auspicious sign, renewal, eternity

Owl: evil, bad omen, wisdom

Pagoda: spiritual progression, counter-balanced surrounding influences

Peacock: eyes of Bodhisattva Guan-Yin, immortality, beauty, grace, dignity

Pear: purity, justice

Pearl: purity, beauty, feminine

Peony: riches, honor, love, affection, beauty

Phoenix: resurrection, revival, sun, fire, peace, prosperity

Qilin (Unicorn or Dragon Horse): mythical creature symbolizing longevity, benevolence, happiness, fertility, honor, wisdom; only male has horn.

Rosary: Buddhism

Ruyi: implies "as you wish" in Chinese; symbol of prosperity, dharma (Buddha's teaching), guidance, longevity, self-defense

Sea: possibilities, subconscious

Snake: the sixth order of terrestrial branches, rejuvenation, fertility, protection

Square: stability, success

Sun: yang energy, God, deity, divinity, heart, eye of God, life force, sovereignty, royalty, fame, balance

Swan: beauty, faithfulness

Swastika: the heart of Buddha (as seen on Buddha's chest), mystic knot, sun

Swiftlet (Swallow): prosperity, abundance, good luck, happiness, vitality, soul mate, freedom

Sword: wisdom, truth, destruction of evil or wickedness, religious symbol (along with spear, ax, sword, scepter, etc.) denoting the conquering of human emotions

Thunder: divine voice, spirituality, knowledge, creation

Tiger: the third orders of terrestrial branches, dignity, power, courage, yang nature, said to ward off demons and evil spirits. (An amulet of a tiger's claw can calm fear.)

Tortoise/Turtle: longevity, endurance, supportiveness

Talisman and Amulet: protector of bearer. (Traditional Chinese charms are made of religious characters written on yellow or red strips of paper for pasting on walls and doors to dispel unwanted spirits and attract good fortune. However, they're also made with other materials and symbolic images or characters. Jade charms are notably and readily available Chinese novelty shops.)

Ten Celestial (Heavenly) Stems: The ten yin and yang of the five elements, combined with the twelve terrestrial (earthly) branches to form a sixty-year cycle

Three Happiness Stars: God of Happiness, God of Abundance and Wealth, and God of Longevity, associated with the Great Bear constellations

Trees: Wood element, expansion and growth, shelters for gods, fairies, and spirits

Twelve Terrestrial (Earthly) Branches: the twelve animals in the Chinese zodiac

Triangle: protection, divinity, abundance, power, energy

Vase: purity, serenity

Water: one of five elements, yin energy, purity, cleansing, renewal, emotion, reflection

Wheel: sovereignty, the cycle of life as depicted in Buddhism's Wheel of Truth

White: purity, spiritual, divinity

Wind: divinity, spirits

Willow: humility, gentleness, kindness, good omen, dispels evil spirits

Wolf: extortion, greed, demon, evil, deceit

Yin and Yang: The Taoist (tai chi) ultimate symbol representing the origin of all things, balance, masculine and feminine principles, union, and perfection; a good omen

Representation

Abundance: fruit trees, rat, goat, swiftlet

Academic Achievement: the four signs (lute, chess, literature, and painting), light, written scroll, owl, book, elephant

Anger: volcano, storm, thunder, lion

Authority or Sovereignty: sun, wheel, official seal, ring

Beauty: pheasant, swan, partridge, peacock, cat, pearl, peony, orchid, roses, lotus, peony

Benevolent: angel, Asian dragon, elephant, jade, pear

Bravery: leopard

Career: water, metal crafts, images of professionals or industries

Compassion and Caring: gods, birds, cocks

Courage: qilin, Asian dragon, tiger, leopard, koi fish, cricket, number nine, horn, rooster

Creativity: playful and colorful arts, crafts, and games; music; children; the color orange; brass Asian dragon sculptures; bees

Divine Power: light, flame, hand, eye, sky, lightning, thunder, wind, mandala, gold

Evil: devil, witch, darkness, Western dragon, fox, wolf, vulture, crow, snake, black cat, owl

Fame: sun, fire, light, candles, the color red, wings, triangle, pyramid, trumpet, bats, magpie, phoenix, pomegranate

Fertility or Offspring: moon, earth, lotus, pearl, spiral, garden, egg, phallus, fruit tree, apple, fig, pomegranate, orange, pear, well, peony, frog, rabbit, snake, emerald, flute

Filial Piety: goat, dove, crow

Four Seasons: spring—Green Dragon, peony; summer—Red Phoenix, lotus; autumn—White Tiger, chrysanthemum; winter—Black Tortoise, plum

Freedom: flaming torch, birds, swallow, butterfly

Good Luck: swiftlet, magpie, qilin, narcissus (water fairy plant), peony, orange fruit

Goodness: deity, angel, light, Asian dragon, qilin, salt

Good News: magpie

Good Omen: high merits for releasing captured turtle, fish, bird, or snake

Health: gentle stream, fresh spring water, clear quartz crystal, jade, ivory, unicorn, coral, pearl, emerald, gourd, earth element, herbs, cherry, bee

Helpful Friends: wing, angel, sky, circular shape, metallic colors, hands, bells

Hope: Bodhisattva Guan Yin, dawn, falcon, green and silver

Humility and Renunciation: saffron, shaved head, joining palms, feet, begging bowl, the color violet, donkey

Joy and Happiness: Happy Buddha, Chinese character *fu*, pink cloud, qilin, magpie, bluebird, butterfly, elephant, persimmon, plum

Justice: Themis (Goddess of Justice), Bao Gong (imperial judge of China), lion, scale, pear

Knowledge and Resourcefulness: images of professionalism, leadership, mentorship, Asian dragon

Lightning: power, energy, fire

Longevity: turtle or tortoise, qilin, crane, deer, bamboo, chrysanthemum, LingZhi (fungus), pine and oak trees, pear and peach trees, vermicelli, mystic knot

Love and Relationships: a pair or two items, mandarin ducks, crane, dove, Asian dragon and phoenix, happy couples, lute, the Chinese character "double joys," rose quartz crystals, vase, red or pink, heart, candles, square shape, earth, rose, orchid, ivy, apple, pear

Loyalty: dog, swiftlet, sparrow, ivy

Marriage: the Chinese character "double joys," knot, songbird or nightingale, dove, peach, plum

Peace and Serenity: vase, dove, olive branch, apple, night

Power: sun, head, arm, hand, Asian dragon, lion, tiger, leopard, elephant, wheel, chariot wheel, triangle, scepter, lightning, fire, ocean

Protection and Guardianship: Queen of Heaven (Ma-Zu), god, goddess, angel, spirit, light, charm, circle, red, knot, pentacle, weapon, bell, multiple heads, eye, open palms, wing, dog (fu dog), tiger, lion, ram, monkey, peacock, garlic, tree, salt, convex mirror

Prosperity and Abundance: goldfish or koi, swallow, rat, water, sailboat, fruit trees, three-legged toad, precious stones

Purity: ivory, jade, salt, diamond, flame, white, lotus, pear

Recreation: egg, wheel, moon, phoenix

Royalty: lion, elephant, jaguar, eagle

Spiritual: sun, flame, halo, white, gold, eye, planets

Soul/Spirit: butterfly, bird, dragonfly

Stability: mountain, pillar, elephant

Strength: elephant, Asian dragon, ox, bear, salmon or koi fish, oak tree, ocean, red

Supreme Being: light, eye, triangle

Transformation: Chinese dragon, fire, water, cave, bridge, frog, butterfly, snake, dolphin, wine

Truth: sun, flame, light, ocean, heart, gemstones, sword, number nine, phoenix

Union: yin and yang, square within circle, joining circle, joining hands, knot

Universe: turtle or tortoise

Victory: horse, lion, phoenix, flag, wing, wreath

Vigilance: eye, rooster, Asian dragon, qilin, dogs

Virtue: fire, qilin, elephant, bee, cow, green

Wealth: God of Wealth, water, gold, koi fish, coin, three-legged toad, elephant, egg

Wisdom: divine angels, deities, lotus, owl, serpent, Asian dragon, elephant, light, water, book

References

Books

Ahlquist, Diane. *Moon Spells: How to Use the Phases of the Moon to Get What You Want*. Avon, MA: Adams Media, 2002.

Andrews, Ted. *How to Meet & Work with Spirit Guides*. St. Paul, MN: Llewellyn, 1992.

Assaraf, John, and Murray Smith. *The Answer: Grow Any Business, Achieve Financial Freedom, and Live an Extraordinary Life*. New York: Atria Paperback, 2009. .

Beer, Robert. *The Handbook of Tibetan Buddhist Symbols*. Boston: Shambhala, 2003.

Chen, Chao-Hsu. *Tao Te Ching Cards: Lao Tzu's Classic Taoist Text in 81 Cards*. New York: Marlowe, 2004.

Chia, Mantak, and Kris Deva North. *Taoist Shaman: Practices from the Wheel of Life*. Rochester, VT: Destiny, 2010.

Cleary, Thomas F. *I Ching: The Book of Change*. Boston: Shambhala, 2006.

Cracknell, James. *Body Science*. London: Dorling Kindersley, 2009.

Dexter, Rosalyn. *Chinese Whispers: Feng Shui*. New York: Rizzoli, 2000.

Finley, Guy. *Letting Go: A Little Bit at a Time*. Woodbury, MN: Llewellyn Publications, 2009.

Gach, Gary. *The Complete Idiot's Guide to Buddhism*. New York: Alpha, 2009.

Gawain, Shakti. *Creative Visualization: Use the Power of Your Imagination to Create What You Want in Your Life*. San Rafael, CA: New World Library, 1995.

Hale, Gill. *The Practical Encyclopedia of Feng Shui*. New York: Hermes House, 2002.

Harding, Jennie. *Crystals*. Cincinnati: Walking Stick, 2007.

Huang, Alfred. *The Complete I Ching: The Definitive Translation*. Rochester, VT: Inner Traditions, 2010.

Karma-glin-pa, Francesca Fremantle, and Chögyam Trungpa. *The Tibetan Book of the Dead: The Great Liberation through Hearing in the Bardo*. Boston: Shambhala, 2000.

Laozi, Man-Ho Kwok, Martin Palmer, and Jay Ramsay. *Tao Te Ching: A New Translation*. Shaftesbury, Dorset: Element, 1993.

Li, Juming. *Hou Nian Yun Cheng: Shi Er Sheng Qiu Gai Yun Fa*. Xianggang: Bai Bao Tou Zi You Xian Gong Si, 2003.

Li, Juming. *Li Juming Long Nian Yun Cheng: Shi Er Sheng Xiao Gai Yun Fa*. Xianggang: Bai Bao Tou Zi You Xian Gong Si, 2012.

Lilly, Sue, and Simon Lilly. *Healing with Crystals and Chakra Energies: How to Harness the Transforming Powers of Colour, Crystals and Your Body's Own Subtle Energies to Increase Health and Wellbeing*. London: Hermes House, 2003.

Linn, Denise. *Feng-shui for the Soul: How to Create a Harmonious Environment That Will Nurture and Sustain You*. Carlsbad, CA: Hay House, 2000.

Losier, Michael J. *Law of Attraction: The Science of Attracting More of What You Want and Less of What You Don't*. Victoria, BC: M. J. Losier, 2006.

Moorey, Teresa. *Working with Hypnotherapy: How to Heal Mind and Body with Self-Hypnosis*. London: Godsfield, 2010.

Palmer, Wendy. *The Intuitive Body: Discovering the Wisdom of Conscious Embodiment and Aikido*. Berkeley, CA: Blue Snake, 2008. Print.

Roman, Sanaya. *Personal Power through Awareness: A Guidebook for Sensitive People*. Tiburon, CA: H. J. Kramer, 1986.

Tolle, Eckhart. *The Power of Now: A Guide to Spiritual Enlightenment*. Vancouver, BC: Namaste Pub., 2004.

Too, Lillian. *Flying Star Feng Shui Made Easy*. Kuala Lumpur, Malaysia: Konsep Lagenda Sdn Bhd, 2007.

Tresidder, Jack. *1,001 Symbols: An Illustrated Guide to Imagery and Its Meaning*. San Francisco: Chronicle, 2004.

Vitale, Joe. *Life's Missing Instruction Manual: The Guidebook You Should Have Been Given at Birth*. Hoboken, NJ: John Wiley & Sons, 2006.

Wang, Biu C. *A Scientist's Report on Study of Buddhist Scriptures*. Translated by P. H. Wei.

Williams, C. A. S. *Chinese Symbolism and Art Motifs: A Comprehensive Handbook on Symbolism in Chinese Art through the Ages*. 4th rev. ed. Rutland, VT: Tuttle, 2006.

Wong, Kiew Kit. *The Art of Chi Kung: Making the Most of Your Vital Energy*. London: Vermilion, 2001.

Wu, Zhongxian. *The 12 Chinese Animals: Create Harmony in Your Daily Life through Ancient Chinese Wisdom*. London: Singing Dragon, 2010.

Wu, Zhongxian. *Chinese Shamanic Cosmic Orbit Qigong: Esoteric Talismans, Mantras, and Mudras in Healing and Inner Cultivation*. London: Singing Dragon/Jessica Kingsley, 2011.

Pamphlets

Yuan, Liao-Fan. *The Key To Creating One's Destiny*. Translated by Chiu-Nan Lai. Houston, 1987.

Yun, Hsing. *Buddhism, Medicine, and Health*. Translated by Kevin Tseng and Mae Chu. Hacienda Heights: Buddha's Light International Association, 2001.

Magazine Articles

Carey, Benedict. "Blind, Yet Seeing: The Brain's Subconscious Visual Sense." *New York Times*, December 20, 2008. http://www.nytimes.com/2008/12/23/health/23blin.html.

Bogo, Jennifer. "Next Gen Digital Sight for the Blind." *Popular Mechanics*, November/December 2010. http://www.popularmechanics.com/science/health/breakthroughs/next-gen-digital-sight-could-cure-blindness.

Storrs, Carina. *Popular Science,* June 2010.

Miscellaneous

Levin, Daniel. Zen cards. Hay House, Inc.

Quotations
Brainyquote.com

A man travels the world over in search of what he needs, and returns home to find it.—George Moore
http://www.brainyquote.com/quotes/keywords/returns_2.html

Do not dwell in the past; do not dream of the future, concentrate the mind on the present moment.—Buddha
http://www.brainyquote.com/quotes/quotes/b/buddha101052.html

Follow your instincts. That's where true wisdom manifests itself.—Oprah Winfrey
http://www.brainyquote.com/quotes/quotes/o/oprahwinfr383372.html

If you can't change your fate, change your attitude.—Charles Revson
http://www.brainyquote.com/quotes/keywords/attitude_14.html

The learning and knowledge that we have is at the most, but little compared with that of which we are ignorant.—Plato
http://www.brainyquote.com/quotes/quotes/p/plato118361.html

The more man meditates upon good thoughts, the better will be his world and the world at large.—Confucius
http://www.brainyquote.com/quotes/quotes/c/confucius386353.html

No problems can be solved at the same level of consciousness that created them.—Albert Einstein
http://www.brainyquote.com/quotes/quotes/a/alberteins130982.html

We can never obtain peace in the outer world until we make peace with ourselves.—Dalai Lama
http://www.brainyquote.com/quotes/keywords/world.html#shUbEe5V5c9dhhUb.99

You must be the change you wish to see in the world.—Mahatma Gandhi
http://www.brainyquote.com/quotes/quotes/m/mahatmagan109075.html

CS.Virginia.edu/~robins/quotes
(Prof. Gabriel Robins's "Good Quotations by Famous People")

Obstacles are those frightful things you see when you take your eyes off your goal. —Henry Ford
http://www.cs.virginia.edu/~robins/quotes.html

Research is what I'm doing when I don't know what I'm doing.
—Wernher Von Braun
http://www.cs.virginia.edu/~robins/quotes.html

The best way to predict the future is to invent it.—Alan Kay
http://www.cs.virginia.edu/~robins/quotes.html

There are only two tragedies in life: one is not getting what one wants, and the other is getting it.—Oscar Wilde
http://www.cs.virginia.edu/~robins/quotes.html

There are only two ways to live your life. One is as though nothing is a miracle. The other is as though everything is a miracle.—Albert Einstein
http://www.cs.virginia.edu/~robins/quotes.html

Whatever is begun in anger ends in shame. —Benjamin Franklin
http://www.cs.virginia.edu/~robins/quotes.html

Whether you think you can, or that you can't, you are usually right. —Henry Ford
http://www.cs.virginia.edu/~robins/quotes.html

Quotes.dictionary.com
As hunger is cured by food, so ignorance is cured by study.—Chinese Proverb
http://quotes.dictionary.com/subject/ignorance

Fear always springs from ignorance.—Ralph Waldo Emerson
http://quotes.dictionary.com/search/Fear_always_springs_from_ignorance

WorldOfQuotes.com
(archive of historic quotes and proverbs)

A journey of a thousand miles must begin with a single step. —Lao Tzu
http://www.worldofquotes.com/search.php?op=search&pagenum=1&query=A+journey+of+a+thousand+miles+begins+with+a+single+step&x=11&y=12

Each man is the architect of his own fate.—Appius Claudius
http://www.worldofquotes.com/search.php?op=search&pagenum=1&query=Each+man+is+the+architect+of+his+own+fate&x=10&y=12

Habits form character and character is destiny.—Joseph Kaines
http://www.worldofquotes.com/search.php?op=search&pagenum=1&query=Habits+form+character+and+character+is+destiny&x=9&y=14

When anger rises, think of the consequences. —Confucius
http://www.worldofquotes.com/author/Confucius/1/index.html

1-LifeQuotes.com
Holding on to anger is like grasping a hot coal with the intent of throwing it at someone else; you are the one who gets burned.—Buddha
http://www.1-lifequotes.com/quotes/keyword/Holding+on+to+anger+is+like+grasping+a+hot+coal+with+the+intent+of+throwing+it+at+someone+else;+you+are+the+one+who+gets+burned.

Luck is when preparation meets opportunity.—Neil Peart
http://www.1-lifequotes.com/quote/3104878

Recommended Websites
ColourTherapyHealing.com
(The healing effect from colors)

FortuneAngel.com
(Information on the Five Elements)

OrganicFacts.net/health-benefits/essential-oils
(Health benefits from essential oils)

Index

t denotes table; *d* denotes diagram

heart attacks, 16, 30
heart chakra, 65d, 67–68, 72
heart disease, 14–15
heart problems, 29
"the heart" (crown chakra), 68
heaven, 24, 26, 43
hedges, 93
Heisenberg, Werner, 6
hell, 27
helpful friends, 176
herbs, 91, 144
He-Tu astrology, 131
hexagrams, sixty-four, 97, 99
higher self, 33, 41, 72
hope, 42, 176
hormones, 49, 62, 68, 115
Horse (animal symbol), 102, 105t, 107, 108d, 109t, 110–111, 130, 172
horses, as pets, 166
hostile stars, 117
How to Meet and Work with Spirit Guides (Andrews), 40, 179
Hsing Yun, 20
huang-qi, 127
Huiyin (The Gate of Life and Death), 66
human, as one of six realms of existence, 26
humility, 176
huo hai (fifth direction), 118
Hurricane Katrina, 31
hurtful memories, 26
hypnosis, 52–53. See also self-hypnosis
hypnotherapy, 50
hypnotic healing, 49–54

images, 143, 147, 151
imagination, 8, 39, 58–59, 68
imbalance
    in body system or organs, 69
    in chakra system, 66
    chemical imbalance, 30, 50–51
    of five elements, 77
immune system, 30, 50, 63, 72
impermanence, 38, 55
impermanence, law of, 23, 28–29
inauspicious numbers, 167
inauspicious stars, 91–92, 128
inauspicious trees, 169
incense, 132, 147, 168
induced trance, 53
infertility, 62
inner balance, 77
inner peace, x, 29, 52, 56–57
inner self, 53
inner struggles, 22, 33, 72, 146
insights, 41
instant gratification, xiii, 45
instinct, 9, 40, 42
intention, xv, 4, 5, 19, 24–25, 35, 38, 41–43, 48–49, 52
interconnectedness, 69
interdependence, 39
"internal feng shui," 70
internal-external energy, 60
Internet, 32, 41
intuition, x, xv, 40–43, 49, 54, 68, 80, 90, 123, 145
intuitive power, 9
intuitive wisdom, 60–61, 68
invisible energy fields/forces, 40, 88, 138

I

I Ching ("The Book of Changes"), 5, 47, 64, 80, 95, 97, 99–100, 110, 131, 172
ignorance, 13, 17–19, 24, 29, 31, 39, 56
ill health, 50
illnesses
    chronic illnesses/diseases, 21, 24, 28, 31, 59
    emotional illness, 52, 62

J

jade, 62, 132, 144, 147, 174
jasper, 62
jealousy, 13, 16, 33
jing (essence), 58, 66, 72
Jobs, Steve, 137
joy, 71t, 176
jue ming (eighth direction), 119
justice, 177

prosperity, 38, 61, 128, 131, 133–134, 147–149, 177
protection, 177
protruding spaces (positive spaces), 125
psychic powers, 58
psychological pain, 72
purity, 90, 177

Q

qigong (chi-kung). *See* chi-kung (qigong)
qihai (sea of chi), 67
qilin (fu dog), 148, 165
qilin (unicorn or dragon horse), 173
quarrel star (star #3), 146
quarrels, 146–147
quartz crystals, 58, 62, 144–148. *See also* rose crystals/rose quartz
Queen of Heaven (goddess of the sea, Ma-Zu), 171
quotes.dictionary.com, 184

R

Rabbit (animal symbol), 100, 101, 106*t*, 107, 108*d*, 109*t*, 110–111, 113, 130, 135–136
rabbits, as pets, 166
Ram (animal symbol), 102, 105*t*, 107, 108*d*, 109*t*, 110–111, 117, 130
Ramsay, Jay, 44
Rat (animal symbol), 101, 106*t*, 107, 108*d*, 109*t*, 110–111, 130, 135
realms of existence, six, 26
rebirth, 15, 23, 27, 44, 61
recognition, symbols of, 150
recreation, 177
rectangle, 165
red phoenix, 166
reincarnation, 26–27
relationship wheel, 107, 108*d*, 109–110
relationships
    afflictive relationships, 109
    building, 109, 111, 118
    Earth elements as affecting, 140

happy, requirements of, 22
having good luck in, 164
how to attract, 145–146
problems with, xiii, 51
representations of, 98, 177
strengthening, 62, 77, 150
threats to, 132, 138
relativity, theory of, 39
relaxation, 52, 63, 70, 145, 151
religion, 17, 26, 36, 40, 55. *See also specific religions*
remedies, 78, 148, 151, 152. *See also* cures
"renewed" year (of buildings), 139
renunciation, 176
repetition, 53
representations, 175–178
resentment, 16, 30, 33, 35–36, 50–51, 132
resourcefulness, 177
restful sleep, 56
rheumatic disorders, 16
Roman, Sanaya, 41–42, 181
romance stars, 145
romantic luck, 108–109, 111, 145–146
rooms
    abandoned, 163
    bedrooms, 89, 118, 145, 151–152, 167–168
    considerations about, 89, 167–168
Rooster (animal symbol), 103, 105*t*, 107, 108*d*, 109*t*, 110–113, 130, 135
rosary, 173
rose crystals/rose quartz, 62, 145–146, 152
rosemary oil, 63
royalty, 177
run-ins with the law, 146–147
ruyi, 173

S

sacral chakra, 65*d*, 67, 72, 151
sacred bowl, 61, 170
sainthood, as one of six realms of existence, 26